Big GamMott

# Hunting Tales

# in the early 1900s
## by Russell Mott
## aka "Double Barrel"

(From articles *in Forest and Stream Magazine*
and transcribed and edited by his grandson,
Graham M. Mott, author of *Hooked by Fly
Fishing: Feel-Good Stories of Family and
Friends, Mishaps, and Mayhem.*)

***Big Game Hunting Tales***
Copyright ©2025 Graham M. Mott
Golden Shadows Press

These stories were first published in *Forest and Stream Magazine.* All downloaded clipart was free except for the cover clipart which was purchased through Etsy.com. Although the publisher has made every effort to ensure the accuracy and completeness of all the information contained in this book. I assume no responsibility for errors, omissions, or any inconsistencies herein.

Attention businesses, corporations, non-profits, schools, and more: quantity discounts are available at the author's cost per book plus shipping costs for sales promotions or fundraising. For more information, contact: Graham M. Mott, Golden Shadows Press, grahammott@hotmail.com or 303-239-0661.

## Table of Contents

DEDICATION..........................................5

INTRODUCTION.....................................7

A MOOSE BY MACHAN..........................11

AFTER CARIBOU ON THE BARRENS OF
NEWFOUNDLAND, 1914........................27

OVER FRED BREWSTER'S WALL..........105

HAROLD AND THE GRIZZLY, 1919.........151

A HEALTHY APPETITE.......................175

AFTERWORD: MY ANCESTORS............187

Big Game Hunting Tales        Russell Mott

# Dedication

(By Graham M. Mott,
grandson of Russell Mott and editor)

I want to thank my mother. Aimee G. Mott for collecting my grandfather's articles and scrapbooks. With her invaluable help, I can publish these wonderful big game hunting stories,

Second to my grandfather, Russell Mott aka "Eagle father," for writing his hunting adventures for *Forest and Stream Magazine.*

I must mention my great grandfather, John G. Mott, who joined his son, Russell, on several hunts and wrote his own remarkable story of a big game hint in Wyoming in 1900. This book is now available as a book, *Monarch of the Glen.*

I would be remiss if I did *not* mention my uncle, Cutler Mott, who as a young boy accompanied his father, Russell while hunting mountain sheep in Canada. I knew and loved Cutler during my childhood.

Finally, to my mother's brother and my uncle, Ed Graham, who was a successful and creative marketing executive and cartoonist in New York City. I used his cartoon of a man sitting in a chair reading a book as my logo for Golden Shadows Press.

# Introduction

It was my mother, Aimee` G. Mott, who obtained my great grandfather's and grandfather's hunting stories from the early 1900s. My great grandfather, John G. Mott, joined his son, Russell, on a couple of these hunting expeditions. Russell, who is my grandfather, also included his young son, Cutler, on a mountain sheep hunt in Canada.

My great grandfather John G. Mott, my grandfather Russell Mott *aka Double Barrel*, and my father, Grenville Mott, were outdoorsmen, well-educated and writers. They had no grammar check, spell check, or iPad to help edit their stories.

I am truly amazed at my ancestors' writing skills. Their stories only required a few minor corrections and changes. I did take some license by editing, adding chapters and paragraph breaks, clipart, photos, and a book title to make these stories more enjoyable for the reader. The photographs are from my grandfather's scrapbooks. I used my iPhone to take photos of these pictures.

Russell's descriptive words of places and people are exceptional. It was such a pleasure for me to transcribe and edit his stories from *Forest and Stream Magazine*.

My ancestors have just been waiting to be heard. Their voices are now speaking through me. The fact that I was the one who received their stories seems preordained. I am publishing a series of three books: *Monarch of the Glen: A True Adventure Story of a Big Game Hunt in Wyoming* –

*1900* by John G. Mott (my great grandfather), *Big Game Hunting Tales from the Early 1900s,* and *More Big Game Hunting Tales from the Early* 1900s by Russell Mott aka *Double Barrel* (my grandfather).

When I look back over my life, it is remarkable that at the age of thirteen I attended a Skinner Brothers camp for boys located near Pinedale, Wyoming, the Wind River Mountains and the Green River. During the camp, I took a week-long pack trip by horseback into the Wind River Wilderness. There is a strong possibility that my great grandfather, John, and my grandfather, Russell may have hunted in this same area mentioned in John's book, *Monarch of the Glen: A True Adventure Story of a Big Game Hunt to Wyoming - 1900.*

Plus, I attended and graduated from the University of Wyoming in Laramie. During college, I also spent two summers working in Yellowstone National Park.

It is evident that I received my own love of adventure, the outdoors, fly fishing, and writing from my great grandfather, my grandfather, and my father. My father wrote many newspaper articles as a sportswriter under his byline, *Beyond the Pail* and a three act play titled, *Heavy Bombardment,* about a B-52 Bomber Wing in 1945.

I have written and self-published two books, *Scams, Swindles and Rip-offs* in 1993 and my most recent book in 2024, *Hooked by Fly Fishing*: *Feel-Good Stories of Family and Friends, Life lessons, Mishaps, and Mayhem.*

I know you will enjoy reading Russell Mott's adventure and hunting stories as much as I did. After 100+ years, relish his words.

Warmest regards,

**Graham M. Mott** (grandson of Russell Mott, transcriber, editor, and publisher)

Big Game Hunting Tales    Russell Mott

# A Moose by Machan, 1908

# By Double Barrel

The fall moon that comes nearest the first of October brings with it the height of the hunting season for moose and consequently, the best of the hunting season. Later comes the snow which closely rivals the rut. Between these two seasons comes the last two weeks in October which are likely to give barren hunting in the New Brunswick woods. As the rut is over, the old bulls are wary, and most of the fools are dead. Generally, ice has formed on the ponds and dead waters. The bulls are on the high beech ridges indulging in pleasant and tender memories of the last full moon.

Yet, despite the disadvantages of the season, the 17$^{th}$ of October found me starting a two-week hunt with Adam Moore on the little Tobique River in New Brunswick, Canada. The weather had turned warm. Two days of hunting convinced us that we had a better chance near the water than on the ridges. On the 19th after working over the ridges in the morning, we visited a lick at noon which Adam had discovered during the past summer. It was located about three miles back from our camp on the Tobique River and consisted of a small pond or mudhole about twenty-five feet wide by fifty feet long. This spot was in the depths of the forest surrounded by thickets of young firs and spruces. From every direction, muddy game trails led into it. The water and mud in the hole seemed to have no distinctive qualities, but something about it was evidently attractive to the moose.

## Log Platform

When Adam first discovered the lick, he was confronted with a problem. It was impossible to lie in wait anywhere near the hole without the moose seeing or scenting a hunter before he could get a shot. To obviate this difficulty, he built a platform of logs in the top of a large yellow birch tree near the edge of the hole. A rough ladder led up it and formed a first-rate imitation of the machan* of East Indian hunting stories. The height of the machan prevented the scent from getting low enough to warn the moose while the hunter commanded the entire hole and its approaches. *Editor's Note: Machan is a platform (as in a tree) used for observation in hunting.*

Though this hole was evidently a resort for moose, the machan had not been a great success. Although Adam had tried it on various occasions, he had never seen a bull at the hole. Yet when we visited it, every appearance promised there were moose. Many of the bushes near the water were broken by a moose hooking its rack. The water in some places was still muddy where moose had been tramping at night. About fifty feet away, a desperate fight between two moose had evidently taken place a few days previously. The ground was tramped and torn, all the small trees and bushes were broken down and large wads of black and gray hair was strewn on the ground. This indicated that some damage had been done.

After looking over the situation, Adam and I retreated at once as quietly as possible. We planned to return toward evening and fought the need to sit down on the machan. Accordingly, after lunch and another fruitless hunt over the ridges, we took the trail back to the lick. I was carrying the little double barrel eight-millimeter rifle which had proved such a success on mountain sheep. I was anxious to test its effect on a big bull moose.

## Moose

When Adam and I approached the water hole, it was about 4:30 in the afternoon. After arriving, we crouched behind a log and saw a spiked bull moose standing in the water. Adam and I watched this moose for a minute or two. I was troubled with an uncertain feeling that the bull had only one large horn. Suddenly Adam whispered to me, "There's a big bull behind the little one. I see his horn. Come on." We crawled onto a game trail which led down to the hole behind a screen of small fir trees. Adam and I were within fifty yards of the water when we heard a terrific rushing noise and splashing in the hole and saw the rear of a moose vanishing in a thicket. Whether this was the big bull or the spike, we could not determine. It was certain that both moose had not seen us or heard our moccasins on the soft ground, so they must have scented us even though it was perfectly calm.

This was most discouraging situation. When moose are badly frightened, they will often leave a waterhole for a week or more. Still hoping they might return that evening, we mounted the machan and sat patiently for an hour and a half. It was no light task to sit perfectly quiet for an hour and a half without moving, speaking or solacing your nerves with tobacco.

Personally, a couple of long trips to New Brunswick in 1907 and 1908 had taught me the great art of sitting quietly on a log. At last, it grew nearly dark, and as there was no sign of any moose, Adam and I climbed down and started back toward our camp. As soon as it got too dark to walk, we lighted a lantern Adam had brought for that purpose and stumbled our way back into camp.

The next morning, Adam and I got up before daylight and walked back to the hole by dawn. It had been undisturbed by moose since the night before, so we left and devoted the middle part of our day to once again tramping over the ridges. Four o'clock in the afternoon found us back at the hole. As no moose were visible, we climbed into the machan and sat down to wait.

Soon after, Adam and I heard a faint noise of something moving through the thicket. Presently the noise ceased. Adam whispered that a moose had evidently been standing close to the hole. Probably upon hearing us arrive, it had quietly sneaked away. This was far from cheerful news and seemed to put a pall on our chances.

## Noises

As there was no wind, the silence was perfect except when a red squirrel engaged in building a nest. This squirrel tore off a fresh piece of bark and ran dragging it through the leaves and bushes making a loud noise out of all proportion to its size. Finally, as it grew darker, even the squirrel ceased all his activities.

Adam got out his watch which showed 5:20. I folded down my peep and threw up the open sight on my rifle. Just as I was beginning to worry whether I could see the front sight at all, the silence was broken by a clear, loud clank. No words can really describe the sound. It was unmistakable, and I knew at once that a big horn had struck against a tree. Adam whispered, "It's a bull and close."

Then for an interminable period, there were no sounds. For at least twenty minutes, we did not move a muscle as the bull was evidently standing listening with his ears. Finally, we heard his horns strike again. Once again, this was followed by a long silence. It was quickly getting dark, and the last light was nearly gone. The fir trees looked black against the pearl-gray sky, and on the ground, only large objects could be distinguished.

The sights on my rifle were invisible. Suddenly, the moose moved again, evidently in the thicket close to the open space. The next moment we heard a loud "ker-whackety bang, ker-whackety bang" as the moose proceeded to hook a small tree to pieces. This was followed by two deep coughing grunts.

## Bull Moose

Suddenly, the moose stepped out into the open about twenty-five or thirty yards away. He was an enormous black shape of distorted prehistoric outline, and from his head rose two great gray horns like sails. The moose stopped broadside toward me and turned his head directly toward the machan.

Let the man who thinks it's easy to shoot a rifle in the dark try it sometime and realize the uncertainty that attends it. I attempted to look down the barrel as best I could, and the night was suddenly torn with the roar of my heavy rifle. The muzzle fire showed in the dark, and the bull went down with a crash.

At once, Adam and I climbed down from the machan and ran to the bull, I fired two more shots into him at point blank. We raised the moose's head and counted twenty-four points on two broad symmetrical blades. Adam produced a little tape which showed over a fifty-two-inch spread. We left my huge moose where he lay and returned with light hearts back to our camp with the aid of the lantern.

Adam and I returned the next morning and found the moose's head just as we had remembered it. The extreme spread of the antlers was fifty-three inches with none of the flatness which makes many smaller moose have large spreads. This moose originally had twenty-five points, but one big brow point was broken off probably in a recent fight. This bull had evidently been through a frightful battle. There were two large holes through the skin of his head and both badly matted. His neck beneath the skin was terribly bruised, and one of his forward ribs had been newly broken. As this bull was unusually large and massive, I would have liked to see the condition of his opponent.

Adam and I found that my first bullet had struck him high in the base of the neck splintering the backbone and cutting the arteries beneath the vertebra breaking the front shoulder. No second shot was needed. My successful moose hunt was over.

**The End**

Big Game Hunting Tales    Russell Mott

## After Caribou on the Barrens of Newfoundland, 1914

A story of a trip which was attended by some excitement and ended in success – big Game Hunting at its best!

**Double Barrel**

*"In the fall of 1903, as I was sitting in my tent on the Gander River in Newfoundland having my tiffin, my guide came to the door of the tent and said that seven caribou were crossing the river just below. I went out and looked them over, and as there were no stags among them with over forty points, I reproved my guide severely for having disturbed my tiffin and returned to finish it. A moment later, he again disturbed me by saying that there were five stags about to cross the river just opposite the tent. So, I again left my tiffin and went to the door from where I shot three stags, one of fifty-five points, one of fifty points and one with fifty-three. Being very satisfied with the day's sport, I resumed my tiffin."* (*Tiffin* is lunch.)

Those who desire to read an account of a trip to Newfoundland with the words indicated above will find numerous books written by British officers and explorers. If, on the contrary, the reader desires an account of what happened in Newfoundland in the fall of 1914, let him read the following pages and certain differences will be apparent.

I

*Nevermore will the great herds cross*
*the deep, worn trails in the barren moss,*
*And the hunter's muscles flag and tire,*
*ere thy lone stag drops to the Mauser's fire.*

Newfoundland is one of the untouched wildernesses which still lie close to civilization. The railroad and fishing villages merely touch the edge of the country. The entire interior is a wilderness practically unexplored with roads or trails and can only be reached by canoeing and walking with packs. As there are practically no horses in Newfoundland, the pack sack and canoe are the only means of reaching the interior.

## Our Guides

As night came on, the train turned and began to cross the southern part of the island. About half past two or three o'clock in the morning, my friend Smith and I were called by the porter. The train stopped, both of us and our bags and bundles were tossed out at the crossing of the Terra Nova River. We had taken precautions to dress in hunting rig when leaving North Sidney and have all our stuff packed.

I was devoutly thankful to find our guide, Dan Burton, waiting in the dark with a lantern by the railroad track. Smith and I gathered up our rifles, two pack bags and a bundle containing a tent, a folding stove and sleeping bags. We lugged them down to the river where Dan had already set up camp. Smith and I found a tent with hot tea and baked beans waiting for us. Dan introduced us to the rest of the party. This consisted of Dan Burton's son, Piney Burton and two Sweetapple brothers, Ned and Tom.

Dan was a big swarthy woodsman of about fifty. His face was lined with a thousand wrinkles from years of exposure. His son, Piney, was a boy of nineteen or twenty, six feet tall, with a clean pleasant face and a figure like Apollo. Ned and Tom were both stocky woodsmen decorated with scrubby beards, short pipes and perpetual grins. The whole party looked satisfactory to me. Dan voiced his impressions of Smith and me by saying it looked as though we meant business and had brought the right stuff along.

After tea and beans, we smoked our pipes and walked up and down the edge of the river watching the stars gradually grow dim until the sky begin to show color in the East. We visited the camp of a Mr. Reed, who had also left the train at Terra Nova. We found him getting ready to start up the river with Bob Saunders, an older guide. They were riding in one big canoe. Saunders looked so old that I wondered whether the trip would not be too hard on him. He spoke with a peculiar cracked, quavering voice. I asked Dan if he did not think Saunders might be too old to be guiding hunters. He replied, "Uncle Bob is pretty old, but he's tough," so I judged Dan was not concerned about him.

When it became light enough to see, we loaded three canoes, pushed off and started rowing up the Terra Nova River. There were three miles of river and six miles of lake travel. By the time we disembarked on a sandbar at the head of the first lake for lunch, my shoulders and arms ached with the unaccustomed work using the canoe paddles.

I was surprised that I had not seen any caribou coming down along the edges of the lake. Through the years of bitter experience, I judged that this was like the fishing resorts where the fishing had always been good either the month before or last year, or those hunting places where the game disappears for some mysterious reason when you arrive.

Surrounding Terra Nova Lake were bare rolling hills covered only with grey rocks and blackened stumps of burned timber. When we reached the river above the lake, we found it lined with spruce and birches. The fall leaves were still swinging on the trees on the border of the river making the changing views as beautiful as any of the other rivers of Northern Canada.

## Canoeing

Soon after lunch, we moved our canoes into the swifter part of the river. At some heavy rapids, I got out and walked along the bank and shot the first game of the trip which was an ordinary snowshoe rabbit of the north. The rest of the afternoon, we worked up the stream sometimes paddling, sometimes pulling the canoes along the bank with a rope and sometimes poling them.

Toward evening, we arrived at the place where we were to leave the river. There, at the inlet of a little brook, we made camp, set up our tent and ate rabbit for supper. As both Smith and I had sore shoulders from the long, hard paddling. Tt felt as though our shoulders had been pounded by clubs. We were tired and glad to turn in for the night.

The weather the first day had been clear and crisp. During the night, I was awakened by the patter of rain upon our tent. When I looked out the next morning, I found a low, gray sky, a steady downpour, and a typical wet, fall day in Canada. After breakfast, Dan came by our tent and told Smith and I that in his opinion, it was too wet to break camp.

Dan and the boys would take a load of stuff and go over and leave it at a camp on the other side of Pynsent Lake. Smith and I spent the day reading, shooting at a target and fooling around the camp. About four o'clock, just as the rain stopped, Dan and the boys returned.

## Tea

The next morning was clear, and we prepared to make our first pack trip into Newfoundland. Piney presented us with the most awful cup of coffee at breakfast that I have ever had the misfortune to taste. I asked him what he made it from, and he produced a can which stated on the label that it was a mixture of chicory and coffee. The makers of that compound should never have boasted in any way. They might have put one bean of coffee in the can, but that is doubtful. I told Piney that this awful tasting coffee was one thing he did not need to pack,

Afterwords, everybody stuck to tea which was excellent and plentiful. During the whole trip, we were deluged with rain and tea. In fact, it is not an exaggeration to say that we were always wet from rain outside and tea within.

Both Smith and I had pack bags for all our superfluous personal stuff. When I left Chicago, it seemed to me that I had taken everything I needed. I had packed my bag with an extra change of clothes, socks, shoes, tobacco, pipes, glasses, two books, a camera, and a few other odds and ends. I found that I had everything I wanted to carry.

## Wet and Spongy

At first, we bore diagonally away from the river over the long marshes. These marshes were entirely different from the muskegs* of the west. In fact, this ground was different from anything I had ever walked on before. While hunting snipe, I had walked through marshes which are mud, grass and water. *Editor's Note: Muskeg forms where permafrost, clay and bedrock prevent moisture from draining. Water* *collects and forms stagnant pools and vegetation.*

In Newfoundland, there are endless depths of wet moss so that walking on them is like walking on layers of wet bath sponges. Each sponge is as wet as it can be, and you sink in up to your ankles at each step. After a rain, the sponges may be a little wetter, but the extra water makes little difference.

Dan, Smith and I had proceeded hardly a mile across these marshes before I was perspiring. My arms and legs also ached from the walking and the weight of carrying my pack. Even the rifle I carried seemed to be heavier than usual. I took one look at Smith and saw he was in much the same condition that I was in.

I was wondering whether we were going to keep walking all day when Dan threw off his pack and said he guessed it was about time to have a blow. We all sat down and rested. As far as I was concerned, it was a perfect time to stop.

After the next mile Dan, Smith and I rested again. While we were sitting still, a solitary caribou cow came out of the woods and walked through the marsh about fifty yards from us. She apparently was not frightened. We looked this caribou over carefully until she eventually walked off across the marsh.

We pushed on to the edge of Pynsent Lake where we had lunch and left our outfit to be rafted across the lake. Dan, Smith and I started walking over the marshes. Smith carried his Mauser while I took my spare gun which was of German make having two twelve-gauge shotgun barrels and a thirty-forty rifle below. We walked around the lake on the high ground over the marshes for many miles seeing no game except one English snipe.

## Wilson Snipe

I was very surprised to see a Wilson snipe so far north on the twentieth of October as I thought that snipe started their southern migration much earlier in the fall. I shot at it when it rose and missed it triumphantly with both barrels. This sighting made me feel right at home in Newfoundland. I have always noticed that in shooting snipe when I am fresh in the morning, I have a good chance for success. However, in the afternoon, at the end of a long and muddy tramp, the odds are in favor of the elusive bird.

Dan, Smith and I spent the afternoon walking on wet sponges while working around Pynsent Lake. After cutting through about a mile of scrub timber, we finally arrived back at our camp. Piney, Tom and Ned were already there and had succeeded in setting up the tent. They were staying in a small log cabin already built for themselves. It was a comfortable camp located in a little tree grove near a brook. Soon a fire was crackling from our folding stove, and I immediately rigged lines to hang up my wet clothes and socks.

## Hair Seal Boots

During the whole time I was in Newfoundland, I never came in without being sopping wet from the waist down despite my popular footwear. All the guides in Newfoundland wore boots made of hair seal skin. These boots are made by the Eskimo women of Labrador and are about the height of an ordinary short rubber boot. They are as soft as a glove and can be easily turned wrong side out. The tops tie just below the knee and make an ideal footwear for the country being soft, light, and waterproof as anything can be. I do not think these boots could be improved on in any way. They owe their waterproof quality to the seal oil in the leather, but when you remove them and turn them wrong side out at night, these boots smell to the high heavens.

Smith stuck to wearing a pair of regular New Brunswick pack shoes. I adopted a pair of the Eskimo boots and wore them during the rest of the trip. However, as I generally succeeded in sinking at least one boot during the day and filling it with water, I never could keep my feet dry.

Hunting Season

The first morning after our arrival at the Pynsent Lake camp was the official opening of the hunting season. Dan would be my guide while Smith went with Ned Sweetapple. Our camp was supposed to be near the edge of caribou country. We hoped to find a good head of antlers.

Dan and I climbed two or three hundred feet above the camp to a broad, high marshland. All the Newfoundland country in the Terra Nova district has the same characteristics. These consist of rolling countryside with broad flats of brown moss-broken strips of spruce and birch. Sometimes the timber can be thick, or it is merely little bunches of scrub spruce.

When Dan and I had covered about two miles and a half, we sat down to rest and Dan lit his pipe. He had hardly begun smoking when a caribou stag with a doe and fawn came out of the woods near us and started walking across the marshes. The stag was a good-sized beast but too small to be worth shooting. He seemed to have good brow points but no tops at all to his horns.

Dan and I followed these caribou for about a mile and cut through the woods coming out close to the stag. He was startled and ran off across the marshes making a beautiful sight with his light body and dark grey head. The stag left the doe and fawn which showed us that the rut was over.

### Camera

From there, Dan and I walked on for three or four miles until we came to a favorable place to watch for caribou. We made a fire, boiled a pot of tea, and ate a substantial lunch of bread and butter, cheese and sardines. Dan and I had hardly finished our meal when a small stag and two fawns came trotting across the marsh to within thirty feet. All three animals stopped and stood looking at us for a long time before they finally grew frightened and ran.

It was bright sunlight with the sun behind us when I remembered to my disgust that I had left my camera at the camp. During the whole time I was in Newfoundland, this was the only time I had a chance to take a picture of living caribou at close range in good light and did not have my camera with me. However, I was not too worried about it because I thought we might see a stag every few minutes.

After lunch, Dan and I worked in a circle back toward camp and saw several cows in the distance but nothing that interested us. About the middle of the afternoon, we sat down to rest. I was searching the distance with my glasses and picked up a caribou near some woods about a mile away. I passed the glasses to Dan, and he said it that it looked like a good stag. I took the glasses again and happened to get a side view of the caribou and saw what appeared to be large horns.

At once, Dan and I started running after the stag. This caribou was bearing diagonally across the marsh toward the woods. We wanted to cut him off. I think we must have run at least three-fourths of a mile. By the time I had gone a half mile, I was going through all the agonies of dissolution. The marsh was particularly soft and full of holes. I went plunging ahead going up to my knees every few steps. I don't think even at my best speed that I could make better than five miles an hour. At the end of three-fourths of a mile, Dan and I were still six hundred yards from where the caribou had disappeared into the woods. There was nothing to do but sit down and recover our breathing. Dan was so tired, and I was literally reduced to a pulp.

We rested for several minutes and then walked over to where the caribou had been. The stag had only four hundred yards to run compared to our three-fourths of a mile. I think if I had been sure that the caribou was going to run into the woods, I might have tried to turn him with a shot. I had no idea what this caribou was going to do until he was gone. Like the big fish that gets away, I have always had a sickening feeling that this caribou was bigger than any other we might see on the entire trip. Perhaps, if I had gotten closer to him, this stag's majestic size would have decreased materially.

At any rate, he was long gone. There was nothing to do but put my gun over my shoulder and start walking back toward camp. It was getting late, and we still had eight miles to go. The last two miles felt like it was getting longer and longer, my legs ached, and my rifle was heavier and heavier.

It seemed as if Dan and I would never get back to our camp. When we arrived, Ned was smoking his pipe and drying his socks before the fire next to the tent. He and Smith had seen only half a dozen caribou cows and one small stag.

After supper, Dan told us that we would move our camp the next day six or eight miles further away. From there, he thought we would find the best caribou hunting grounds. As I had seen three stags the first day, it seemed to me it should be relatively simple to kill my legal limit of three stags.

II

*The longest shot kills the smallest head*
*The big head falls without work or skill,*
*The perfect shot with the perfect head,*
*Long have we sought and are seeking still.*

The next morning was cloudy and looking like rain. Even though we were only walking about six miles, we packed up everything and started walking toward the high marsh in the general direction of Millais Lake. The guides were, of course, heavily loaded even though we left most of the supplies at the camp with the expectation of sending a man or two back for food when we needed it. After two day's rest, I found I could carry my pack and rifle more easily.

## Shooting a Stag

We had walked together for about two miles and then sat down to rest. I stood up with my pack still on my back while looking over the marsh. I saw three cows and a big stag moving across it about four hundred yards away. These caribou would pass about three hundred yards from us, and there was no cover.

I called out to Smith that there was a stag, and he should shoot it. He replied that it was my stag since I had seen it first. As the stag proceeded across the marsh, Smith and I continued to argue on the subject while Dan danced up and down and begged somebody to shoot. Finally, Smith said the caribou could get away as far as he was concerned. It was my caribou, and he was not going to shoot it under any circumstances. Smith doubted he could hit the stag even if he did shoot at it.

As it seemed hopeless to continue this argument, I ran ahead of Dan until I got a good view of the caribou and sat down with my rifle. I was using my German double barrel chambered rifle for the Adolf Newton Express bullet. *Editor's Note: The .30 Newton cartridge was designed by Charles*

*Newton in 1913. Newton originally called the cartridge the 30 Adolph Express after Fred Adolph, a well-known immigrant gunsmith*

As my rifle was high velocity and shoots the Spitzer soft nose bullet, I paid no attention to the elevation but just pulled the trigger. After firing the first barrel, the stag jumped into the air and started away from me on the run. I fired the second barrel instantly and staggered him. The caribou was evidently badly hurt but kept on moving at a good gait. The stag was getting further away every minute, and my next three shots had no effect. I started running after him and gaining on him when he suddenly stopped and swung broadside to look back. I was about the same distance as when I first fired at the stag but this time, I killed him with a shot through the lungs.

On examination, this stag proved to be quite a disappointment. He had long, tall horns much like an elk, but few points, only nineteen in all. While he was a fine-looking animal, he did not have the sort of head that I had hoped to get in Newfoundland. I was determined that I would be more careful before I fired at another caribou stag in the future. Dan seemed satisfied, however. He said that he knew it was not a great head, but it was plenty big enough for my first caribou.

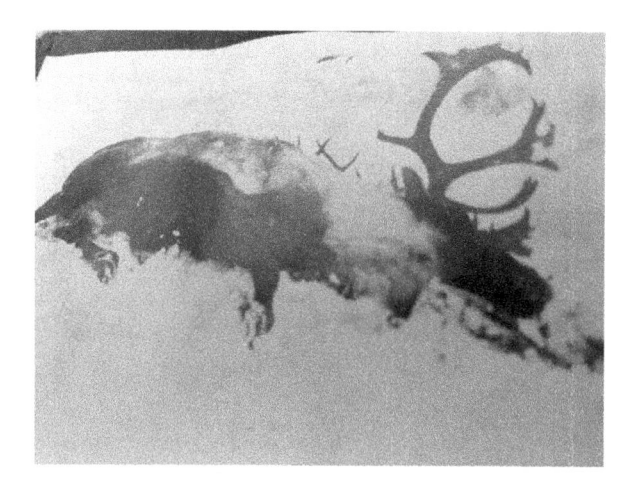

## Wet the Stag

We had lunch there and took out one bottle of our limited supply of Scotch to wet or celebrate the stag. What our party did to a quart of Scotch in wetting a stag was something awful. I knew that the four bottles we had brought with us on this trip would not be more than sufficient for wetting six stags. As for any idea of drinking a hot Scotch every night when we came in wet, that sweet dream had vanished. When one of the boys left to get more grub, he would take the caribou's head back to the other camp on the river.

## Permanent Camp

After lunch, all of us pushed on four miles. The latter going was difficult as the marsh was particularly soft, but finally, we began to go downhill. After finding a brook which ran down through a heavily timbered valley, Dan stopped and announced that we would camp here. There was a little fireplace already there and a place for the guide's lean-to, but absolutely no place to put our tent.

I have never seen a worse camping ground. It was mossy, rocky, bumpy, and wet. All of us set to work digging out stones and pulling up moss. We managed to make a level nine-by-nine plot by piling two feet of boughs on top and raising it above the dampness of the ground. As this was to be our permanent camp, it still was not a good location for our tent. Ned found a big, black thin rock in the brook which made a stand for the stove so that it would not set fire to all the moss.

It was evident to me that by this time we were in good hands. Every one of our guides were good-natured and always willing and ready to do anything in their power to make our trip a pleasant one. In the past during various my hunting trips, I had been accustomed to taking care of my own camp. This included setting up the tent and the stove. I was always more than glad to do it.

Our camp was certainly comfortable after a tough day's hunt. These guides were anxious to help us and apparently considered it their duty. In the woods, it is entirely a matter of choice how much the guides care to do for you. If they help you hunt, set up the camp and cook your meals, that is all you can really expect. At the same time, there are a thousand and more things which the guides can do if they choose. Dan and his men certainly went the extra limit for Smith and me.

On previous colder trips where a morning fire was a necessity, it had always been our custom before turning in to decide who should make the fire in the morning.

The first night in our main camp in Newfoundland, Smith and I played bezique* for the championship of Terra Nova with the understanding that the loser would light the fire in the morning. Smith was victorious so I filled my hat with kindling and a box of matches and crawled into my sleeping bag with the chilly prospect hanging over me.
*Editor's Note: Bezique is a French 19$^{th}$ century card game for two players.*

In the morning, I was awakened by a gentle popping noise from the stove and found that Tom had just finished lighting the fire. He was telling Smith that breakfast would be ready in twenty minutes. Of course, this was a tremendous luxury and totally unworthy of a Roman. Nevertheless, I turned over in my sleeping bag and resigned myself to such good treatment. Smith was peevish that he had not rooted me out before Tom arrived. It was no consolation to him that his turn was coming soon.

## Smith's Caribou

The next day broke cold and windy with the temperature below freezing. Ned and Smith started off toward the marshes and the edge of Lake St. John. Dan and I headed more for the hills with only a few little marshes. The walking was much easier although the stones were hard on my soft boots. It was cold and raw as a harsh wind was blowing.

There seemed to be no signs of any caribou. I could not tell why, but for some reason I had lost faith and did not believe there were any caribou in the area. I told Dan we might as well return to camp and did so without seeing any signs of game in the seven or eight miles that we traveled. We arrived

back in camp about noon. After having lunch, I went into the tent, smoked my pipe, and read my book, *Barchester Towers.*
*\*Editor's note: Barchester Towers is a novel written by English author, Anthony Trollope, and published in 1857. The book delves into the politics of British church society and focuses on the lives, ambitions and power struggles of its characters.*

About three o'clock, I heard voices and coming out of my tent. I found Ned and Smith had come back with a caribou head. It was a twenty-five-point head with one big brow point and two big bays and the horns running to a point with no points at all. This caribou was a handsome trophy, and Smith was very pleased.

Ned and he had been eating lunch when they saw three caribou come out on the marsh about a quarter of a mile away. They both had crawled and stalked the animals across the marsh until they got within two hundred yards. Just as Smith was about to shoot, a flock of wild geese came winging their way over the marsh honking loudly. While the stag stood gazing at the geese, Smith fired at him three times and with the third shot, the stag collapsed in a heap on the marsh.

The bullet had struck it in the forehead knocking out the front of the brain. It was a beautiful shot for killing effect, but as Smith was shooting at the middle of the body, he did not feel particularly elated. Ned thought he had overshot the stag every time. We found that Smith's rifle was sighted so high that it unquestionably would shoot over a caribou at any reasonable range.

The average big-game rifle is likely to be sighted too high as the manufacturer seems to feel that this makes people believe the rifle has a longer range. The proper way to sight a big-game rifle is to shoot it off-hand on a dark day in bad light at one hundred feet and sight it so that it will shoot point blank at that distance. On that theory, you will miss less game for it is the tendency of amateurs to shoot high when excited or in a hurry.

At any rate, Smith had his first head and a good one at that. He was pleased and so was I. After all, I was the one who had induced him to come on this trip and was especially anxious that he shoot a caribou stag.

Smith's day was long and hard, and he was tired. The tendons in the back of his legs also troubled him considerably, swelling in lumps just above his heels. This was probably caused by the fact that he had changed from heeled shoes to heelless boots so suddenly.

## My Second Stag

Smith decided that he would take a day off to rest his hurting feet. The next morning, Dan and I started walking toward the same ground where Ned and Smith had hunted the day before. We went about three miles toward Lake St. John and then through a region heavily timbered with scrub spruce, birch, and spaces of open country.

Dan and I had not gone far into the timber when we came upon a small stag standing by himself. This caribou ran out of the woods suddenly having winded us, stopped and stood looking to see what the trouble was. Soon afterward. we passed a lone cow or doe that raced off at full speed. It was interesting to watch the caribou running fast over the marshes. The soft spongy going did not seem to bother them at all as they moved with a swift pacing gait occasionally breaking into a full run for a few bounds.

Next, Dan and I came upon a small marsh in the woods perhaps three hundred yards long and one hundred yards broad. Standing at the upper end of it were three doe caribou and one small stag. We stopped behind some bushes and worked our way to about seventy-five yards from them. I took out my camera hoping for a picture but before

I could snap one, they caught sight of us and started off on the run. These caribou were as wild and shy as deer. I guessed they had been hunted previously.

From there, we turned off through the woods and walked across another little marsh. We were nearly across it when I turned to look back and saw a caribou on the far side just poking his head and nose out of the woods. I whispered to Dan, and we both crouched down and waited until the stag came into plain view. He had a good head of antlers. I let him walk out until he was opposite me at about one hundred yards away. I shot the first barrel into him as he stood, and the second as he sprang and fell dead.

Dan and I found both bullet holes behind the caribou's shoulder not more than three inches apart. This stag had a beautiful and symmetrical twenty-eight-point head with two good brow points, symmetrical bays and tops. In fact, he had satisfactory antlers. I was pleased even though this caribou's horns were not as large as I had anticipated.

At once, Dan and I made a fire, had tea, and cooked some caribou meat which we had carried with us in our pack.

Skinning the Caribou

Dan started to work cutting off the head and skin. In skinning, beside the robe and head, he also removed the shanks which was new to me. Dan skinned about three inches above the knee joint of the back leg down to the dew claws and slitted it over the knee joint in the back carefully. When the skin was taken off the bend at the knee joint, it made a natural heel. By sewing up the front, these shanks would make a perfect pair of moccasins. The guides kept them to wear on top of their seal boots during the winter. I had never seen these anywhere else.

A soft, wet snow had begun to fall. Dan stopped to set two fox traps near the carcass. I carried the lunch sack, glasses and my rifle, while Dan held the stag's head on his shoulders. It was a long, hard hike back to camp because of the snow. We had to stop to rest on the way, build a fire and make tea.

### III

*When you find your back*
*is aching from the pack,*
*As you start to feel a trembling in the knee,*
*When you see a mist arise*
*that begins to dim your eyes,*
*Then it's time to boil a kittle of tea.*

Back at camp, we found Ned and Smith had taken a short walk but had not seen any caribou. They were disappointed in not seeing any animals. Smith's heels were feeling a little better so he thought he could possibly hunt the next day.

## "Bruise"

That night, we ate the Newfoundland national dish for the fourth or fifth time for supper. It consisted of fried salt pork, cod fish and hard bread boiled together in a general stew. Hard bread is soaked for twenty-four hours until it softens and is cooked with the cod fish and pork. This is called "Bruise" and is a thoroughly filling dish. I have no doubt it would be a hit on a fishing or sealing schooner but personally, I much preferred eating caribou steak.

The next morning, the 26$^{th}$, Ned and Smith started hunting in the country where I had shot my stag. Dan and I were determined to go over to the bare hills where we had formerly been. Tom and Piney went back for more food at the main logging camp and carried out the two caribou heads.

Dan and I tramped all day but found nothing except partridge berries to eat and two ptarmigan which we were not successful in killing. Toward the end of the afternoon, we saw one solitary caribou doe and fawn on the marshes, but they were wild and gave us no chance to take any pictures. Dan kept repeating that during the year before all this ground had been filled with Caribou. Now, it seemed as if most of the animals had left the country.

On our return to camp, we found that Smith and Ned had merely gone down to Wallace's look-out, a low hill not far from Camp. There, they could overlook a large extent of the country. They had seen only two or three cows and no stags.

It was almost dark when Piney and Tom returned to camp with fresh supplies and two partridges which they had shot on the road. These birds made a satisfactory supper.

Dan and I decided that tomorrow we would go back to the big marsh where we had previously hunted. Ned and Smith would walk as far as they could toward Millais Lake.

*Frances, Louise, and Anna Maria*

Our camp, by this time, was very comfortable. Tom had put three or four more layers of boughs under our tent, and Dan had moved his bed into it. We also had two caribou skins on top of the floor cloth. and had set up drying lines, candle sticks and all the paraphernalia of a permanent camp. I read, talked, smoked, played cards in the evening, and fed the folding stove untold quantities of green birch.

Smith had named the stove "Frances" after some mythical lady in his past because it was entirely beyond human control. It either refused to burn at all or roasted everybody out. This became a popular joke with the guides, and I think it gave us permanent reputations as humorists. At least, when we left, I know that they had named their two other stoves, "Louise" and "Anna Maria" respectively, according to their female characteristics.

## Pictures

The morning broke dark and cold with a sharp wind. Dan and I started walking over the marsh and had gone about three miles when I spotted the head of a doe sticking out behind some trees at the neck of the woods. I called Dan's attention to it. We crossed through the woods and crawled behind some little bushes where we spotted three does and a stag feeding. This stag was a beautiful creature with a big, white mane, but his horns were too small to be of any interest.

I got out my little camera and took several pictures before the caribou ran off. The pictures came out well, but the caribou were just bits of white on the plate because we were over fifty yards way. This distance was just too far away to do any distinctive work. These caribou started running to leeward. After going about a mile, Dan and I looked up to windward and saw them crossing the marsh two miles ahead of us. They had swung a five-mile circle in the same time it took us to walk about a mile.

We tramped all day around the edges of the big marsh getting back to camp late in the day without seeing any other animals. Smith and Ned arrived even later that evening. They had gone over toward Millais Lake, and although they had seen seventeen caribou, none of them had horns or were worth shooting. Smith was totally exhausted after his long day of hunting.

At this point, our hopes of further success began to look bleak. Smith's heels now had two bunches the size of hickory nuts on his tendons, and he could hardly walk. To add to our discouragement, Dan said he thought there were just a few caribou in this part of the country and possibly no good stags.

After consulting with Dan, we decided to take the floor cloth of our tent, move up about seven miles further toward Millais Lake. Dan and I could put up a lean-to there from which we could hunt. Smith preferred to stay in the main camp and rest his sore legs and feet.

I still felt somewhat confident of shooting my third caribou stag. I realized, however, that it would be impossible for me to pick and choose. Under these conditions,

I decided that I would shoot the first respectable head that was offered.

## Trappers

Accordingly, the next morning, Dan and I started toward Millais Lake with the floor cloth and a pack of bedding and provisions. I had my sleeping bag which consisted of an oil silk cover with a camel's hair blanket and an eiderdown quilt inside it. It was a good bed, light and warm.

Less than two miles from camp, Dan and I suddenly came on the body of a caribou cow lying with her back torn out and fox traps set around it. Dan was furious and said that there had been some strange trappers in the country spoiling his hunting and killing the caribou. He thought this was probably the reason there were not more caribou. In fact, it seemed the consensus in Newfoundland that the high prices paid for fox furs had caused an increased amount of trapping and illegal killing of caribou for bait. For this reason, most of the animals had been driven farther into the interior.

## Fox Trap

Dan and I had further proof about an hour later. We were moving toward the place where Smith had killed his first caribou. While walking along a caribou trail, I heard a crash next to me. My first thought was that I had stepped on and broken a bottle. On further investigation, I found that I had stepped into a fox trap set in the middle of the trail. It was unconcealed without bait and certainly would never have caught even the most foolish of foxes. Who had set it and with what vain hope, Dan and I had no idea?

About six miles further on, we picked out a camping place in a grove of spruce and birches. Dan and I to put up the lean-to and then started walking across the marsh. We went directly to the place where Ned and Smith had seen the caribou the day before and saw four doe and a small stag. Then, Dan and I pushed on across a high ridge with a broad marsh on top of it. We saw no caribou, and as it was getting late, turned homeward. Almost at once, a cold, persistent rainy downpour set in.

Just as Dan and I were thoroughly soaked, we saw a small caribou stag with some does and caught sight of a big grey stag walking the marsh about six hundred yards away. We ran for all we were worth about a quarter of a mile and crouched down behind some little spruce trees. The caribou was coming directly toward us across the marsh. When the stag came to within a couple hundred yards of us, Dan and I noticed that he was a handsome beast with only small horns. I took out my camera and focused it as best I could even with the hopeless weather conditions.

The stag continued walking slowly across the marsh, feeding as he came and making straight toward us while the rain continued to pour down. He approached within thirty feet of our hiding place and was about to pass ten feet from our left when he suddenly caught sight of something suspicious behind the bushes and stopped. He stood there and stared with the rain drops running down his face. I watched through my small camera aperture in the bushes while the water ran down the back of my neck and began to soak the bellows of my camera.

After only a few minutes which seemed more like an hour, it became perfectly evident that the stag intended to stay and look at us forever. I feared my camera would be ruined and jumped up behind the bushes. I did this suddenly with the same effect as if a person had opened a jack-in-the-box before an unsuspecting child. The stag jumped straight into the air and if he could have screamed, he certainly would have done so. It seemed almost as if he jumped as high as his own shoulders and then turned and bounded across the marsh. I took one picture, but the weather was so bad that when it was developed, the stag merely showed up as a grey blur.

After this caribou disappeared over the horizon, Dan and I kept walking to the place where we had seen some other caribou earlier that morning. It was getting dark and was still raining hard when we came upon a bunch of six or eight caribou with one stag. Dan and I moved closer to them and looked them over carefully with glasses. I was somewhat in doubt as to whether I could shoot the stag. Since this stag did not have a good pair of antlers, I decided to spare him.

## Soaked

On arriving back at our camp, Dan and I started a roaring fire in front of our lean-to. We were soaked to the skin but managed to dry our clothes by hanging them under the roof of the lean-to. Our underclothes dried quickly from the heat of the fire which was about eight feet long and as close to the lean-to as was safe. The dishes consisted of a frying pan, a tea pot, one plate, cups, spoons and our sheath knives. With these, Dan made a hearty supper of fried bacon, caribou meat and pancakes. He mixed the batter for these in a birch bark pan which he had carved earlier in the day. After this stylish meal, we smoked our pipes until our clothes were dry and went to bed with the rain still pounding on the roof of the lean-to. I thanked heaven that the floor cloth was waterproof and slept soundly.

## Foggy

Next morning, it was still raining when we had breakfast but quit shortly afterwards. Dan and I started out for a full day's hunt. Unfortunately, a fog had set in, and we could not see more than two or three hundred yards ahead of us. Where we had seen the last stag the night before, there were a couple of cows standing in the marsh. Dan and I were not sure if there were any stags with them, so we sat down on a little hill and waited for the fog to lift. To pass the time, I ate my fill of partridge berries which were plentiful nearby.

An hour later, the fog finally broke, and since there were no stags, Dan and I started walking up a ridge toward Millais Lake. It was a hard pull, and we were soaked to the skin by the wet bushes which deluged us as we pushed through them. When we reached the top of the ridge near the lake, we spotted two caribou cows crossing the marsh half a mile away.

In a few moments, they ran over the crest of the ridge, and a big stag appeared out of the woods a quarter of a mile in front of us. Evidently, he had been disturbed by the cows I passed my glasses to Dan, and he reported that the stag had long, straight spikes for horns but was of no value.

As this seemed to be a pretty good place for caribou, we decided to eat lunch. Dan succeeded in getting some dry wood and started a fire burning in the marsh. We made tea and cooked caribou steaks. I took off my boots, wrung out my socks and tried to dry them in front of the fire.

## Drinking Tea

The motto of the Newfoundland guides should be "Tea and Plenty of It." At breakfast, everyone had three or four cups of tea. When hunting, we always stopped early in the day, built a fire and had two or three more cups. If the return trip to camp was going to be long, we would stop three or four miles from camp and have a few more cups.

As soon as we arrived in camp, we always found the tea pot on the fire. Everyone had another round of tea, and of course, there was plenty more for supper. In addition to this, if anyone found time passing slowly, the first thought was to boil the water in the kettle and have tea. Considering the good health of our party and the large amount of tea we consumed; I believe any evil effects of drinking too much tea are grossly over-exaggerated.

## My Third Stag

After lunch, I put on my foot gear, and Dan and I started walking toward Millais Lake. We went down the side of a ridge, around the edge of the lake and back toward home. It was getting late, and I was beginning to feel tired and ready to rest. I wanted to kill my third caribou though I began to feel I might hunt for days without seeing a respectable head.

I was plodding along looking first at one foot and then the other with my mind a perfect blank when Dan suddenly said, "There goes your stag." In front of us were two small peninsulas of woods which ran out on each side of the marsh about three hundred yards from us.

Right across the middle of it, a caribou stag was moving at a fast-ambling gait and sailing through the marsh as though it was walking on hard pavement. Dan said excitedly, "Shoot him, shoot him, you will never get any closer!" I said, "I don't think I can hit him at this long range."

I sat down in a mud puddle and raised my rifle and let go, holding high and in front of the caribou. The stag paid no attention to my shot, so I fired again aiming at the top of his head. At the second crack of my gun, he collapsed in a heap on the marsh.

When Dan and I reached him, we found that the bullet had struck the base of his neck and broken the bone. He had a good twenty-three-point head with two brow points and beautiful tops, but unfortunately. his bays were poor.

I was so glad to get my third caribou which completed my hunting. I was satisfied with this stag although sorry not to have killed a larger head. Dan skinned out the head and shanks. Since the rut was now over, this stag did not smell musky. We filled our knapsack with meat. I carried the knapsack, glasses, axe, and rifle while Dan managed the caribou's head and robe on his shoulders.

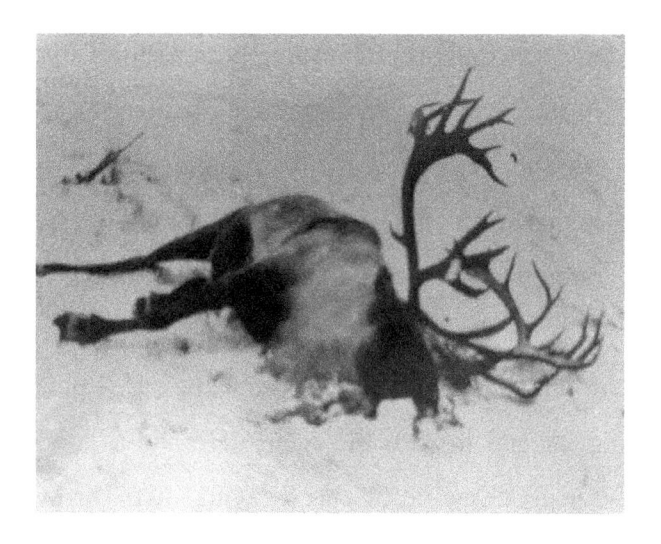

I was already tired, cold and wet when I shot this caribou. Now I had to carry a heavy pack on my back so that by the time we reached the lean-to, I was worn out. I know Dan had a good test himself.

Tom had placed logs up along the sides of the lean-to. Everything was in good shape. We had a good, hot supper and dried our clothes next to the fire once more. It felt so comfortable that we stayed up until at least eight-thirty. Darkness set in at five, and when you are through eating your supper by six, there is nothing to do but talk and smoke your pipe until bedtime.

## Stories

It was amusing to hear the conversations of Dan and Tom during the evenings. Like all inhabitants of Newfoundland, their greatest interest and most of their talk is about the sea, of trips after codfish or seals, and of the different schooners and the men who commanded them.

Here is a sample of one conversation. "You know that Bill James, the one that lives at Alexander Bay and has got seventeen children? The first time I saw him he came aboard the schooner named Mary, looking for a job as cook. He had a pair of whiskers that he could almost tuck in his pants. I said to him, 'You would make a hell of a cook with them whiskers in the gravy.' He came back the next day all shaved, and I never discovered it was the same feller and hired him. He didn't like the job. The next day when we were anchored, he stole one of the dories, rowed away, and we never saw him again that trip."

The next morning, we left Ned resting at the lean-to while Tom and I went back to the main camp. We left early and arrived at the camp well before lunch. I went into the tent and filled my pipe full of tobacco and read my book, *Barchester Towers*. I never moved that afternoon or evening while reading except to poke the fire and have supper. It was pure pleasure to rest after ten days of difficult hunting. I was satisfied to know that I had three caribou heads and was perfectly content to not shoot any more. Even if my heads were not exceptionally big ones, at least I had no misses and was satisfied knowing that I had located the stags myself.

I decided to stay in camp the next day and rest. Tom made a large trough on legs out of the trunk of a tree and filled it with plenty of hot water and did the family washing for the trip. This included every one of my clothes except the few I wore for the sake of modesty. As the tent was full of drying clothes, it was hot enough so that wearing many clothes wasn't necessary. I gave my guns a thorough cleaning, sharpened my knives, and did a thousand other things that can be done around a hunting camp.

By evening, I was thoroughly rested. When Ned and Piney came into the tent for a smoke, I suggested that we all go down to the log camp the next day. While they took the caribou heads out to the river, I would stay around camp and try to catch a few trout.

## Ptarmigans

The next morning, we started walking without any baggage whatsoever except my sleeping bag. The guides had some bedding at the log camp, and there was plenty of food there. Piney took a twenty-two-caliber rifle while I carried my three-barrel gun with a half dozen shells.

It was not too long when I saw several ptarmigans ahead of us on the path. I walked to within fifty yards and decided to not go any closer and shot at the ptarmigan on the ground. As ptarmigan are a rare treat in Newfoundland, I resigned myself to this simple form of pot hunting and fired all six cartridges into the bunch. At the end of the fusillade, all six birds were lying quietly on the ground. We walked over to pick them up when four of the wounded birds started flying off across the marsh in a different direction.

It was the most disgusting thing I ever saw. Every twenty yards, they seemed about to drop and then would take another spurt. Ned said that every one of them would be stone dead when they struck the ground. Since I had no more shells, I could only curse and watch most of our dinner disappear. Finally, I gave up and picked up the two ptarmigan that were dead.

I suppose there might be some judgment for shooting at the birds on the ground. I confess that I regarded it strictly from a pot-hunting basis because I wanted some ptarmigan to eat before I left Newfoundland. Later that day, we came upon three more ptarmigans. Piney succeeded in stalking and shot one with his twenty-two. This gave us three birds. It was the only other time in Newfoundland that I saw ptarmigan within shooting distance and never saw more than fifteen birds during the whole trip.

## Trout Fishing

We reached the log camp about eleven o'clock and had lunch there. Ned and Piney each took one of the caribou heads and started off walking toward the river. I had not brought my fly rod, so I cut a spruce pole, added a piece of string, a hook, and a little meat and walked up to the brook about a mile from the outlet of a small lake. I started fishing for trout there. When the trout stopped biting, I had caught sixteen fine fish. These fish averaged from six ounces to about three-fourths of a pound in weight.

There was no sign of Ned and Piney at camp. I cleaned the trout, washed the dishes, made a fire, boiled myself a pot of tea, and sat down to smoke. It was almost dark when they finally arrived. Ned admitted he was tired, but Piney seemed fresh as a daisy. Such is the difference between a forty-five-year-old and a twenty-one-year-old. We ate trout and potatoes for supper and turned in on the floor of the log house and immediately all fell asleep.

## IV

*Back to the city streets,*
*Back once more to the grind and strain,*
*Still, I feel the moss 'neath my feet,*
*And the smell of the barrens wet with rain.*

Smith did not want to hunt caribou anymore. His heels were so sore that he could hardly walk, wanted to rest one more day and would leave the next.

Though the caribou hunting had been poor as far as finding big heads, I felt that the trip was probably more enjoyable than if there had been more caribou. After all, we had to hunt long and hard for our stags. Newfoundland differs from any country in which I have hunted because there is not much game available except for caribou.

In New Brunswick, when you are through shooting moose, you can hunt deer. In the western states and practically all other countries, there were always some other kinds of game which you could hunt when you had secured your main trophies.

## Animal and Bird Life

In Newfoundland on the Terra Nova, there is absolutely nothing else to shoot but Caribou. There are not even partridges and rabbits in sufficient quantity to count. When you're through hunting caribou, your trip is over. The country itself is barren of other animal life. There are not even squirrels in Newfoundland, and the woods are silent without them. Of the other animals, we saw only three rabbits.

Also, you will only find a few birds. We saw two or three camp robbers or moose birds, a few partridges, and perhaps a half dozen other birds during our stay. Were it not for the caribou, Newfoundland would be a country lacking much animal life.

We spent one more day in our main camp resting and getting things ready for our trip back to Terra Nova. The next morning a heavy rain began. Dan suggested that it would be wise to stay in camp another day while Ned and Tom carried all the extra stuff up the river. This trip was about seven miles so that Ned and Tom decided to spend the day in the rain carrying out the caribou skins and heads while Piney took care of packing things around the camp.

Dan said he would like to go out and shoot a caribou for himself. If he was successful in shooing one, he would give us a piece of the caribou meat to take home. We had not been able to carry any caribou meat from to the lower camp, so Smith gladly gave Dan his rifle to use. I spent my day trying to catch more trout. Dan returned at dark after a successful hunt with the hind quarters of a small stag, some pieces of tenderloin, and the skin. He told us that he would be delighted to give us the hind quarters. Smith and I were glad to have it but had no idea how we were going to get the meat home or how to preserve it.

## The Silver Fox

During the day, Dan had visited the camp of two trappers and found them to be the sorriest and angriest of men. It seemed that they had caught a beautiful living silver female fox which was worth close to five thousand dollars for breeding purposes on a fox farm. The trappers had made a stout pen of logs and put the fox in it with some caribou meat scraps to eat and then left to check their other traps. Upon returning, they found that a bear had visited their camp and knocked the pen down to get at the caribou meat. Of course, the fox and their fortune had disappeared through the first hole in the pen. No speculator in Wall Street who sees his millions melt away in a panic was ever hit by a worse fate than these two woodsmen.

Ned and Tom did not get back until late and were tired from their long, hard trip. Dan never seemed to mind how much work Ned and Tom did. Before the end of the trip, our stock joke was to say, "Let the Sweetapple twins do your work." They kept at it morning, noon and night and never complained. Smith and I were so glad to have them on our hunting trip.

## Back to Terra Nova

The next day was partly cloudy. We planned to leave the river that day. It was the last of the week, and unless we caught the train that left Terra Nova early Friday morning, we could not get out of Canada until Monday. No trains ran on Sunday in Newfoundland or the eastern part of Canada. We knew that it would take a long full day of walking and rowing to get back. We started about six in the morning carrying our heavy packs and guns toward Pynsent Lake.

Once at the lake, we loaded the raft and discovered that it would not hold all of us. Dan and I decided to walk while the raft was poled four miles down the edge of the lake. The walking was difficult along the steep sides of the mountain leading down to the lake over small shrubs and fallen timber. In addition, it began to snow heavily and got worse as we went along.

Dan worked his way through the timber at top speed and reached the lower end of the lake just about a minute before the raft arrived. We were still four miles from the river. Putting on our packs, we started walking across the marsh. By ten o'clock, we arrived at the river and made a fire. Dan got out the last bottle of whiskey, and everybody had a drink of hot Scotch. We put all our stuff in the canoes and started rowing down the river toward Terra Nova. We paddled fast the first six miles and arrived near the entrance to the lake about noon and stopped on a sand bar.

## Lynx

While the rest of the party was eating lunch, Dan set a lynx trap on the ground near us. I have since heard from him, and he said he went back and found a big lynx caught in his trap. Dan had seen the tracks of the lynx while going up and coming down the during our hunt. He decided that this area must be lynx's regular haunt.

We had a lunch of ham, beans and dough boys. The latter had to be cooked twice because Piney filled the pot too full so that when it boiled over, it extinguished the fire. It also burned the Sweetapple twins and most of the food. Piney's second attempt at cooking was more successful.

At half past one, we finished lunch and started canoeing down toward Terra Nova Lake. A head wind was blowing, splashing the water over the bows of our canoes. For about three hours, we put all our strength into paddling. By the time we reached the bottom of the lake and moved into the river, I felt as if my arms and back were nearly broken. Smith also looked like he was in agony.

As soon as we beached the canoes at Terra Nova, Smith and I jumped out and started walking toward the station house as fast as we could go. We hoped to get some

letters and news from home and the latest account of the War. When we had left on our hunting trip, the battle of the Aisne* and a big battle along the Russian frontier were proceeding. We hoped for good news.
*Editor's Note: The Battler at the Aisne was trench warfare between the Germans and the Allies during World War I from September 10 to the 13$^{th}$, 1914.*

At the railway station, we found the station agent's father standing in front of the stove. He seemed to be a well-informed man and told us that as far as the war was concerned, nothing much had happened except that Turkey had joined to fight in the War. Things were much the same as when we left. It seemed impossible to us that nothing had changed during the three weeks we had been out of the world.

## Terra Nova

This was the first time I noticed the metropolis of Terra Nova. On one side of the river was a deserted sawmill and four or five tumbled down houses whose sole purpose was to furnish Dan with boards to make crates for our caribou heads and meat. While on the other side was a big, dilapidated shack.

At one end of this shack lived a section hand with several dirty looking children. In the rear, lived the station agent in one little room with a telegraph instrument, a chair, a stove, and a bed. There was nothing else but a sea of mud and the railroad track. Luckily, we found one or two letters awaiting us and gladly abandoned the slush of the station house and went back to read them in our tent by the river.

Meanwhile, Dan was still crating the heads. We had supper and sat down to wait for our train which was not due until two in the morning. The evening passed slowly, and we had tea and another supper at eleven o'clock in the evening. Although we had walked seven miles and paddled another seventeen that day, we all sat around the tent, smoked and told stories until near the train's arrival. The last two hours were spent waiting for a train which was at least two hours late.

It was half past four in the morning the next day before we said goodbye to Dan, Piney, and the Sweetapple twins. Smith and I were anxious to leave and climbed on board the train for Port Aux Basques with a wooden box containing two hind quarters of caribou attached to the platform of a rail car to help keep it cool. We were glad to be on our way home.

*Tipperary*

It continued snowing hard all the way through Newfoundland and at the Northern end of the Island, Smith and I saw several caribou hunters along the railroad tracks waiting for caribou to cross in migration. We arrived in North Sidney, changed our clothes, packed our trunks, and went to the station to catch the night train to Boston.

Smith and I found the station filled with soldiers leaving for the war front. They were singing *Tipperary.* * The people were shouting and cheering, and the women were crying. It was very exciting, and we watched it all with deep interest until our train pulled out. *Editor's Note: "It's a Long Way to Tipperary" was an English music hall song performed in 1912 by Jack Judge. It was the soldier's marching song of the First World War.*

As we were sitting in the smoking compartment on the train, I leaned over to Smith and putting my hand on his knee said, "It was all very interesting wasn't it. How long do you suppose it would take us before we finally remembered that we left without checking our luggage and boxes?" Our caribou meat, heads, trunks and other paraphernalia were still sitting on the train station platform at Sidney. Such are the horrors of war.

**The End**

# Over Fred Brewster's Wall

Russell Mott with mountain sheep heads

## by Russell Mott

*"I had killed a number of rams before, but none so big and none so far away. As I looked at my prize, I thought this was certainly the climax of sheep hunting."*

There is one hunter's rule that has no exceptions to prove it: the wind always blows in sheep country. At our camp on the Sulphur River in Alberta on the morning of September 8, a gale was blowing down the valley. It brought rain and sleet which beat continually on our tepee. A fog covered the higher mountains, and hunting was impossible. We were marooned inside the tepee and kept a huge campfire burning in the center while our pipes and cigarettes added to the smoke.

Among other subjects, we discussed our hunting plans. Jack Brewster, my guide, said he thought we might just as well start hunting the next morning. We would look for the valley that his brother Fred had described to him before Fred left to inhabit a dugout during the War "somewhere in France."

## Fred's Valley

Fred told Jack that if one followed up the valley in front of where our camp now stood, it would bring one to a place where a view could be had looking into a broad, beautiful valley. There was a lake at one end of it and wonderful sheep country all around. Fred further said that there were always rams in the valley. It was an all-day job to walk to it and included a hard climb.

In fact, according to George Denison, the cook, Fred had told him that he had "a devil of a time" two years before while trying to help one of his sportsmen climb up the wall at the back of the valley. This wall closed the valley three miles from camp and was precipitous and about 300 feet high. It could only be scaled in one place.

Jack and I determined that if the next morning was clear, we would leave George in camp to watch the horses. We would take our packs and rifles and start for Fred's valley. We would hunt until we shot a ram, if there were any sheep to be had.

## Impossible Climb?

The following morning broke fair, and Jack and I started walking. I carried my Springfield rifle and Jack, my Mannlicher, as a spare gun. In our packs, we had bedding, sweaters, tea, bacon, bread, cheese, and a small axe. We left camp about 8 o'clock and at 9 reached the bottom of the wall.

It seemed almost impossible to climb as this wall stretched straight across the valley from one mountain to the other and was perpendicular. On inspection, Jack and I found there were plenty of hand and footholds. After a quarter of an hour's desperate climbing, we finally reached the top.

The back part of the rocky ridge which formed the wall was not nearly as high as the front. There were two gulches that ran up into the mountains, one to the right and one to the left. We had no idea which one would lead to Fred's valley, but the left one seemed more promising, so we started climbing up the creek bottom.

A little stream flowed in the bottom of this gulch. It wound in and out among the rocky peaks sometimes spreading out in little grassy places and narrowing between steep hillsides. All this climbing was far above the timberline. Jack and I kept following this alpine brooklet for hours seeing nothing except two ewes and a lamb which we surprised feeding in the bottom. At first, the sheep did not see us approach. When they did notice us, they rushed with hardly a pause straight up the mountainside to the higher peaks.

At last, our valley narrowed until it ended in a basin surrounded by towering peaks with their sides covered with glaciers and snow. There was one place that was lower than the rest and probably not over a half-mile climb. Jack looked at the scenery and said he guessed we had probably taken the wrong gulch but might as well continue to climb up and look over the top.

It was after 12 o'clock, and I had been carrying my rifle and pack since 8 o'clock. I did not feel like climbing up a half mile to look over some precipice and then return.

However, since there was no alternative, Jack and I toiled up until at last we neared the top.

## The Valley

I confess that it was with fear and trepidation when I looked over the edge but was overjoyed by the view. Before us, there was a precipice with 3,000 feet of broken rock which sloped steeply down into a peaceful valley. To our left, the valley widened to a broad expanse of dark green pines broken by golden patches of poplar trees and a swift stream pouring down the center to a river in the distance.

Nearly opposite where we stood, there was an army of pines where a few groves pushed toward the upper basin of the valley. Beyond and to our right lay a beautiful green and gold meadow with a blue lake gleaming in the center. On all sides, the meadow spread upward over the slopes and terraces of the surrounding mountains until it gave way to the rock and snow on the highest peaks.

If man had been here before, he had left no signs. The timber, the lake and the meadows lay sleeping in the sunlight as if they had slept for centuries. As beautiful as it was, my mind could not be distracted from trying to spot mountain sheep.

The basin at the top of the valley had all the distinctive marks of an ideal sheep range. The steep mountain meadows and the rocky peaks were the promised land we were seeking. The point at which we were standing was about three miles above the valley.

It took an hour of the hardest climbing to reach the bottom. While climbing down, I had to step on the worst kind of rocks. My shoes were cut through in several places. At the bottom, we found a sheltered place in a small bunch of timber and had our lunch of bread, tea and cheese. Jack and I were both exhausted. After that, we sat, smoked and rested for about a half an hour and then decided to take a short walk and find a location to set up a camp for the night.

There was another small clump of pines about a mile up the valley, and Jack and I made our camp there. This was a simple procedure as we found a big tree with dry ground under it and a little spring nearby. We left our packs under this tree and walked to the edge of the timber to inspect the valley once again.

## Billy Goats

Jack and I began to scan the country with my glasses when we saw four goats lying on the rocks about a half mile down the valley. These goats had no idea of our presence. One enormous Billy was stretched over the rocks like a great yellowish-whitish rug lying in the sun. Fortunately for the goats, they were only of academic interest to us at that time.

Jack and I started walking up the valley and had gone only two or three hundred yards when we saw through the glasses that there were five animals grazing on a lower slope of the mountain. We worked up about a half mile from them and moved under the shelter of the last tree.

From there, the glasses showed them clearly which proved to be a bunch of caribou, four cows and one bull. Once more, I had no interest in shooting. However, Jack and I rested under the trees and watched them for a long while.

## Four Big Rams

Jack took the glasses from me and began to look around the landscape. He suddenly gave a gasp and said, "There are four big rams on the mountainside about a mile straight beyond the caribou." I took the glasses from him and looked toward where he pointed. I could make out the four big sheep. When the light was just right, I could even see the curl of a horn. All four were grazing quietly in a difficult place to make a stalk, and it was already about four o'clock in the afternoon.

The wind was blowing down the valley, and there was a gulch directly beyond the sheep. If the wind had been blowing the other way, it would have been a simple matter to go up the gulch to get within easy shooting distance. Above the rams, the mountain was steep and full of a slide rock so any attempt to approach them from above would be difficult and noisy. To walk straight toward them was impossible as they could easily see us. Furthermore, if we frightened the caribou, the goats would probably run straight up the mountainside and scatter the rams.

At first, Jack favored letting the sheep go until the next day. Finally, he agreed with me that it would be better to try and stalk them now. I suggested walking back down the valley about a mile almost to where the goats were located. There, Jack and I could climb up to the same height as the rams and work along the side of the mountainside toward them. We might be exposed in plain view and would have to turn back. However, Jack and I could find ourselves sheltered by the curve of the mountain or a ridge and possibly make a successful stalk. I thought of the previous days of poor hunting and prayed for good luck this time.

By the time Jack and I had come to this conclusion, it was already 4:15 in the afternoon. I had been on my feet for eight hours and felt more like going to bed than starting a hunt. Also, I was haunted by the fact that when I am tired, I usually shoot poorly.

## The Stalk

There was no time to get lost if we were going to reach the rams before dark, so we started walking down the valley. After going about a mile, we started climbing upward toward the rams. Fortune seemed to be with us as the mountainside had a succession of little hollows and ridges for cover.

It seemed likely that the rams must be feeding in a hollow with this ridge between us. If so, our principal worry was that one of the rams would walk out to have a look around the countryside and might spot us. About every two hundred yards, Jack and I stopped and scanned with the glasses to see whether the rams were in sight but could see no signs of them.

I began to feel more and more hopeful of succeeding. We were in plain sight of the caribou during this time, but they never looked up the mountain at us. The goats had long since left for some less crowded place.

We crawled along the mountainside through grass filled with many beautiful wildflowers. Forget-me-nots, asters, Indian paint brush, wild larkspur, and a large blue flower just the color of a gentian* grew everywhere profusely. The sun, which was beginning to set, turned the little lake into a blazing mirror.

*Editor's note: Gentian root is a herb used for medicinal purposes. It grows in the mountain climates of Europe, Asia, and the Americas. These plants have trumpet-like flowers in blue, yellow, and other colors.*

## Eagle

At one point as I came up over a ridge of rock, there was a rush of wings, and a great bald eagle flew almost into my face. I was so startled that I nearly dropped my rifle. The eagle was even more surprised than I was. He banked his tail and wings like an aero plane and with a squawk of surprise, darted straight into the air and whirled up over the mountain. I suppose the eagle had never seen a ferocious looking animal like me at such close quarters.

Jack and I came to a small ridge which separated us from the location where we had last seen the four rams. Jack worried that theses sheep might have moved on to some other place. While he searched the foreground with the glasses, I examined the sights on my Springfield rifle and threw a cartridge into the barrel.

Jack waited while I cautiously crawled up to the top of the ridge and looked over. About two hundred yards beyond, I spotted the four rams who were feeding. All had magnificent heads, and I could not tell which one was the biggest. I crouched below the ridge and waited a couple of minutes until I could catch my breath.

## Shooting

Then I crawled again to the top of the ridge and worked around until I was directly facing the sheep. The rams were still feeding, and one big fellow was standing broadside to me. I rested my elbows on my knees, raised the rifle, sighted at him carefully, held my breath, and pulled the trigger as slowly as if I was shooting at a target.

At the crack of the gun, the ram fell in a heap, and the other three dashed off along the mountain side. As they ran, it was evident that the ram in front was the biggest and most alarmed. He had been shot at before, and the memory was far from pleasant. The other two rams followed him but kept losing ground. I ran across the mountain toward the sheep while trying to keep the other big ram in sight. I kept firing and emptied my magazine with Jack yelling at me to keep shooting at the big one in front. I was excited and out of breath.

## Two Rams

I shoved another clip of cartridges into the Springfield and sat down on a rock to rest. Just then, the big ram climbed on top of a boulder almost straight away from me, and I fired again. As we learned afterwards, the Spitzer bullet struck him just behind the fore shoulder ranging directly forward through his neck and out the center of his forehead. The ram sank slowly forward and lay stretched across the top of a boulder. The other two rams were confused by their leader stopping and turned dashing back up the mountain. I shot no more as I had my two big rams.

I looked at my watch, and it was a quarter past six, two hours since we had started the stalk. I looked around and found Jack busily digging a little hole in some moist sand where there was a trickle of water. I suddenly realized that I was so thirsty. Both

Jack and I had a drink before we went to investigate the sheep.

The first ram that I killed was lying in the grass below us in plain sight and had a fine pair of horns. The second ram showed merely as a tiny grey patch on top of the rocks far above us. I walked down to the first ram and examined him. He had a beautiful head with the horns having a heavy base and a fine curl. When we measured the ram two weeks afterward, the base was 16½ inches and the curl 37 inches. This ram carried his weight well and was about nine years old.

When I left my first ram and started walking toward the second, I was astonished at the long distance. For a time, I began to think I might have lost the ram entirely until I saw Jack cutting across the mountainside above me. He arrived at this ram first and waved his hat because he was very satisfied.

I still had quite a hard climb before I finally reached him.

Afterward, Jack always insisted that I killed my second ram at 500 yards. I make no statements myself but whatever the distance, what a big trophy ram it was! His horns had a base and weight making it a wonderful head. After the head had dried for two weeks, the horns were still 17 ¾ around the base and 38 in length. I had killed several rams before, but none so big or so far away. As I looked at my prize, I thought I had obtained the climax of sheep hunting.

## Skinning the Heads

We had packed the camera on every previous hunt. Unfortunately, this time we had left it at camp so were unable to take any pictures of the rams. However, I doubt if we would have much success anyway as the sun was setting quickly. We were a long way from camp, and it behooved us to make haste. We skinned out the two heads as quickly as possible. Jack took the big one on his shoulders while I carried the smaller one.

Jack and I were already alluding to the other ram as "the small ram," and yet, he was bigger than any ram I had previously killed except one in Mexico. We were forced to leave all the meat except for keeping some liver for breakfast. It was heart breaking to waste such good mutton, but there was no possible way for Jack or me to carry it back to camp. In fact, I still was not sure how we were going to eventually get the two heads back to our base camp as the smaller one weighed forty-five pounds and the bigger one was closer to sixty.

Carrying the Heads

Jack and I started moving down the mountainside with the heads on our shoulders and made quick progress toward our camp and finally arrived at 7:30. Soon, we had a roaring fire started. I broiled bacon on a crotched stick while Jack sliced bread and made tea. We filled ourselves with bacon, bread, cheese, and tea. While we smoked until half past nine, I said to Jack, "If this doesn't make the end of a perfect day, I do not know what does."

There is always the morning after a successful hunt. In this case, it broke cold and windy with the difficult job laying before us of carrying the heads back to our base camp over the mountain and out of the valley. Jack and I set out at 8 o'clock that morning, each with a head on our shoulders and carrying our packs and rifles. We hiked for about a mile. My ram's head was heavy, and although I could have carried it on level ground, I found it almost impossible to climb with it on my shoulders as the weight was so badly balanced.

After a half an hour, I was completely done in and thinking I would be forced to announce to Jack that I could not go any farther. Suddenly, he saved me the trouble by throwing down the heavier head and his pack and said, "I can't carry this damn thing any farther. The weight is all in the wrong place. It trips me up, and I can't see where I am going."

## Two Heads

The situation seemed utterly hopeless to me. Jack floored me completely with the following extraordinary statement: "I do not mind the weight if I could get it balanced right. If you will take the two slings off the rifles, I will make a harness to put over my shoulders and will carry both heads. You can carry both rifles and packs."

Jack fixed the harness so one strap passed over each of his shoulders. One head hung on Jack's breast and the other on his back. It was a very heavy load, but I could console myself with the thought that it was at Jack's own suggestion and funeral. Jack and I threw away practically all the extra grub except some bread and a can of sardines in my pack. I put the field glasses inside my shirt, slung one rifle over my back on top of the pack using the field glass strap and carried the other rifle and pack in my hands.

Jack and I started walking up the mountainside again. We rested every few minutes, and by 12 o'clock, were finally on top. By now, it was blowing a gale. The snow was coming down in sheets, and the wind cut through our clothes like a knife. Jack and I walked down in the snow on the other side until finally arriving at a little creek in the bottom. I broke the ice with my rifle butt. Jack and I wrapped ourselves in our blankets and had a lunch of water, bread and sardines while the snow pelted us unceasingly. My shoes were completely cut to pieces. I was doubtful if they would hold together before reaching the base camp.

After lunch, Jack and I were too chilled to smoke so had to get moving or freeze. We continued our course down the valley making much faster time on the downward grade. By 2 o'clock, we were at the top of the wall and 2,000 feet below where we had been.

The snow had changed to a heavy cold rain which soaked us to the skin. The rocks on the side of the wall were greasy and dangerous. It seemed impossible to get the heads down now, so Jack and I cached them at the top and walked down ourselves. From there, it was a straight one hour walk in the rain back to the base camp

## Base Camp

At 3 o'clock, Jack and I arrived at base camp. George looked at us from the door of the tepee and greeted us pleasantly, "Well, if you two are not the most miserable half-drowned, unlucky son-of-a-bitches I ever saw!" I said, "George, we are probably all of that except the unlucky part but don't worry about that. Just run and grab the rum bottle."

Half an hour later, we were finally warm and dressed in dry clothes. George, Jack and I were eating venison steak, pancakes and baked beans. We washed it all down with hot rum punch and were a well-satisfied trio. That completed two successful days of hunting for both Jack and me. Shortly afterwards, we all climbed into our sleeping bags and were not heard from again until the next morning.

Jack and I brought a pack horse and walked back to the wall. Jack climbed up ahead of me, and I went up part way to a flat place. He lowered the two ram heads to me with a lariat. I was able to catch them both below. By this means, Jack and I were able to get the two heads down and back to our camp. Then I shaved, and George took pictures of Jack and me with my two big ram heads. I was more than satisfied with my accomplishments. Next, we moved on to goat country.

**The End**

Big Game Hunting Tales          Russell Mott

# Getting Your Goat, 1915

**Russell Mott**

I object to making a goat out of a mountain goat. He is a much-maligned creature, though I believe the fault lies chiefly with this animal. For some reason, he has never received the appreciation that is his due from the American sportsmen. The mountain goat is accustomed to having the mountain sheep as his nearest neighbor and is usually hunted as a sort of sideline to the sheep. This goat is entitled to prime consideration and should be given the highest respect.

Long ago the late-lamented Bill Bye wrote:

*"No more in the wilds of Harlem*
*Will I hunt the festive chamois;*
*If I ever do, damois!"*

The mountain goat is denied a fair share of the dignity he deserves. Perhaps one principal reason is why more hunters do not boast of having shot one is they would rather hunt mountain sheep instead.

Many sportsmen do not realize that the mountain goat is not similar in appearance to the barnyard variety though both may be possessed of the same innate deviltry. As a matter of fact, the Rocky Mountain goat is shaped much like a buffalo, weighs about 300 pounds when full grown and is a most dignified and imposing creature.

After the goat has allowed the mountain sheep to pick out the roughest country, he moves next door where the entire mountain is straight up and down and settles himself for a comfortable winter. He is always in the meanest country the Rocky Mountains can provide and generally, is found at the very top.

The goat whiles away his leisure hours on the mansard roof of North America.

For recreation, he "four-steps" along the edge of an abyss of the kind Dore* has portrayed in illustrating Dante. After the goat has scaled the side of an almost sheer precipice, he peers around the corner at the top of the world and positively grins. *Editor's note: Paul Gustave Louis Christophe Doré was a French printmaker, illustrator, painter, caricaturist, and sculptor.*

Add to this the fact that the mountain. goat is harder to get a shot at than anything else except sheep. Now, you have a fair idea of the real status of the Rocky Mountain goat. He is positively the most contrary "critter" in the world and hunting him is no job for a nervous man.

If there is a precipice bordered by a flat top, the mountain goat invariably takes the edge and gaily trots along on juts of rock scarcely big enough for a hat rack. After you have climbed for hours and are winded, shaken and exhausted, you will frequently locate a goat about a mile away on the other side of a ravine that you swear can't be crossed with anything short of wings. There, he stands and looks at you. If your glasses are strong, you can positively see his whiskers wag.

On this mountain goat hunting trip, my father, John G. Mott accompanied me. I had previously told him some things about the Rocky Mountain goat which I had learned from experience. My father declared that he was going to shoot a goat, but I felt that possibility was rather dubious. You see, my father was born in 1839 and enlisted in the Federal army in 1861. A simple mathematical computation will show that he may be beyond the age for climbing a precipice to get a goat.

But my father did it as I watched his performance from a vantage point on the opposite side of the canyon more than a mile away and am quite proud of the feat he accomplished.

## Camping In Alberta

This hunting trip took place in Alberta on the Eastern slope of the Rockies. My father and I rode the Canadian National Railway to Jasper and joined Jack Brewster, who was our guide. We rode horses into the mountains to the headwaters of the Sulphur River.

Our first day in camp was cold and rainy. Jack and I were the only ones to leave the camp. I spent the afternoon with my fly-fishing rod and got wet to the skin. I proved to my satisfaction that there wasn't a single trout in what I thought was a perfectly good trout stream.

Jack climbed the neighboring mountains to survey the goat country and had not returned at dark. Without waiting for him, my father and I and Alec and Ernest, the horse wrangler and cook respectively, sat down to a supper of sheep steaks, potatoes, and onions which Ernest had cooked over the fire in the middle of our big tepee.

We were just finishing supper when Jack came in wet but cheerful. He had seen three big goats on the neighboring mountainside. Jack had located them about three o'clock in the afternoon and watched the goats until they finally laid down at dusk. He had stood in the rain for three hours watching them a mile away. The fringes of Jasper Park are great big game country because of the protection afforded the animals in the park.

## Fog

Imagine our disgust when we crawled out of our tepee the next morning and found everything covered with a fog as thick as soup. To shoot anything even fifty yards away would have been impossible. We ate breakfast and waited until nine o'clock without much improvement. At last, and in despair, my father, Jack and I saddled three of our horses and rode out.

Our path crossed the creek below the camp and led through a beautiful forest of spruce for about fifteen hundred feet. We wound upward in long diagonals, sometimes riding and sometimes leading our horses. At last, we emerged from the forest into high timber meadows. There, to our delight, my father, Jack and I found ourselves in clear sunlight although the valley below was still swathed in heavy fog.

These meadows were in a wide pass between the mountaintops. My father, Jack and I followed a trail for a couple of miles getting to the source of a little brook. We stopped and tied the horses to a tree. Jack announced that from the mountaintop in front of us, we would be able to see the goats if they were still where he had seen them the previous day. My father sat down to smoke his pipe while Jack and I climbed up to the top, crawled to the edge of the canyon and looked over.

## Three Goats

Before Jack and I was an almost perpendicular fissure. On the opposite side, more than a mile away, stood three goats. Inspection with our glasses showed that they were all full-grown males. Now came the problem of how to approach them. It was impossible to cross the canyon above us. Our only choice was to circle around the mountain from where we were and then climb down and cross the canyon far below where it became a valley between the mountains.

We would be out of sight of the goats. Once crossed, it would be possible for us to climb up the other side of the mountain closer to where the goats were lazily feeding. This meant a long walk and climb so we all decided that my father and Jack should make the stalk while I watched them from above through my glasses. This would give me a bird's-eye view of the proceedings.

My father and I carried Springfield rifles cut down to sporting models. Mine was equipped with Lyman sights. Since my rifle was suited to my father's eyes better than his own rifle, I gave him mine. Jack also decided to leave his own Ross rifle with me.

## The Stalk

My father and Jack started stalking the goats about eleven o'clock. I took a drink of water, had a smoke, and then climbed back to the edge of the canyon where I could see the goats.

By this time, the three goats were lying down in a semi-circle about ten feet apart. They were little more than white specks to the naked eye. I kept wondering how close Jack's Ross rifle would come to them if I fired it. I lay watching the goats for a long time and scanned the farthest slope of the mountain with my glasses hoping to see my father and Jack.

Noon came and passed. I went back to the horses, ate my lunch and once again took up my vigil. At about one o'clock, I saw two specks on the rocks far beneath and below the goats. With many pauses, I watched my father and Jack gradually progress like ants up the side of a house. I turned my glasses from them to the goats who still lay peacefully on the rocks.

Finally, affairs began to approach a crisis. I could distinguish my father and Jack plainly. They were moving with the greatest care to not be seen by the goats and were crawling to keep under cover and get closer. I looked again at the goats through the glasses, and they had not moved. One raised his head and seemed to be looking around in a bored fashion.

## My Father's Luck

When I looked again, my father was sitting down with his rifle aimed toward the goats. I said to myself, "Good heavens, he is not going to try a shot at that long range!" With the boom of his gun echoing up the canyon, the three goats leaped to their feet, and each one ran in a different direction. An instant later, one of the goats had disappeared. I could see the other two running up the face of the mountain.

While the sound in the canyon echoed and re-echoed with the reports from my father's rifle, I took Jack's Ross rifle and fired three or four shots at the goat running up the mountainside directly opposite me.

From my first shots, I could not see where the bullets were striking until I saw a spurt of splintered rock fly up after the last shot thirty or forty feet below the goat. I realized that I was simply wasting ammunition. I grabbed my glasses again and continued watching the other two goats.

One goat had run down the side of the canyon and quickly disappeared. The goat, at which I had fired, was gone from the top of the canyon and safe. The third one, plainly wounded severely, was slowly walking up the rocks. Suddenly, the canyon again echoed to the crack of my father's rifle, and this goat dropped and lay motionless.

Yelling my delight, I dropped my glasses, rifle and coat and started to run toward the scene of the kill. I was not concerned about disturbing any game, so I took a much shorter route than that followed by my father and Jack. In about an hour, I was on the opposite side of the mountain and could not see them.

## Skinning Two Goats

I walked back and forth howling like a lost soul until I finally saw a thin wisp of smoke curling up from the bottom of the canyon. A wild scrambled walk brought me down to the bottom. Walking up the canyon, I found my father sitting and smoking his pipe by a fire waiting for some hot tea while just above him Jack was already skinning out his goat. This was the goat that had first disappeared running down the canyon wounded and was out of my sight from my point of observation. The other goat I had spotted was lying dead higher up on the mountainside.

After a triumphal lunch, Jack and I found the second goat, and he immediately went to work on it. I held the goat while Jack cut off the skin. The moment the skin came loose, I let go of the carcass. It started rolling downhill and did not stop until it hit the bottom of the canyon a quarter of a mile below making a small avalanche of stones and earth. It was a good illustration of what might happen to an inexperienced climber if he fell on these precipitous slopes.

## Proud Son

We took a shortcut back to camp. Jack carried one goat skin on his back, while I had the other skin in the pack with the teacups on top. These goat skins are one of my father's most prized possessions. He is seventy-six years old, and though I have hunted big game all over the American continent for the past fifteen years and been lucky, I can recall nothing in all my hunting experiences that gave me as much genuine pleasure or made me as proud as my father's successful hunt. I know a thing or two about how difficult it is to stalk and kill a goat. My father accomplished this rare feat when he was in his seventies.

On that same trip, I also shot a splendid mountain sheep whose massive horns show that he was at least twenty-two years old. This ram was running about 150 yards away from me and going like the famed Irish Banshee* when I pumped about four shots at him and got him. I had also scared up a smaller ram that was running like a gray streak when the big fellow suddenly sprang up. Of course, I let the young one have his freedom. *Editor's Note: Banshee is a supernatural being in Irish folklore who wails or sings as a harbinger of death.

**The End**

# Harold and the Grizzly, 1919

**Russell Mott**

*My Camp in the Hills*
by RALPH GARNIER COOLE

*There's no place that's nearer to heaven*
*Than my camp in the glorious hills;*
*With the wild things around and about me,*
*And the silence that soothes as it thrills.*

*With my fire that crackles and dances,*
*With the perfume of cedar and pine,*
*Where no sound awakens the echoes*
*But the crack of that rifle of mine.*

*Or the snap of a twig breaking silence,*
*As some "critter" goes creeping along.*
*Or the croon of the stream in the canyon,*
*A singing its lullaby song.*
*And when I roll up my blanket,*
*With nothing above me but sky,*
*And am lulled off to sleep to the music*
*Of the pines as they murmur and sigh—*

*Why, I haven't a care in the world, mate,*
*All gone is the worry that kills,*
*And life's just a glad, happy play-day,*
*In my camp in the glorious hills.*

This story violates all the well-known rules of a hunting story. The first of these is that the author should be the principal character. The second is that it should be illustrated with numerous photographs taken on the spot. The third is that it should end with some remarkable kill. And fourth, there should be a picture of the proud sportsman sitting or standing with his unfortunate victim.

None of these necessary elements can be found in my story. In fact, the reader may as well be prepared for the shock of not finding them. At the same time, if he is a fisherman, who is used to having the largest fish get away, or if he is a hunter who retains the memory of degrading misses, I hope there will be something in my story which will appeal to the reader and convince you of its accuracy.

Big game of all kinds is becoming scarcer every year. The grizzly bear has never been protected anywhere by a closed season. These bears have been shot regardless of age or sex and become almost extinct in this, the year of our Lord, 1919. There are probably as many grizzlies in the Canadian Rockies along the line of the Canadian National Railways as anywhere else in America. The districts along the railroad are entirely unsettled with not many hunters, and the country is tough enough to give adequate protection to any game.

On the twentieth of May 1919, I arrived at the ranch of George Denison, twelve miles beyond Lucerne in British Columbia. The officials of the Canadian

National Railway kindly arranged for the train to stop at George's ranch. I got off the train in the heart of the Canadian Rockies and twelve miles from the nearest settlement. In fact, there was no neighbor within twelve miles. George's ranch lay on a little flat plateau, and it was possible to reach game country within a few hours.

## George and Harold

We started our grizzly bear hunt the next morning with an adequate pack outfit of seven horses. George was an experienced trapper and woodsman who knew the country thoroughly. He took with him his nephew, Harold, as a cook who was one of the heroes of the events to be narrated.

Harold had made a peaceful livelihood in trapping until 1915 when he volunteered to go to France in the Canadian

Army to fight the German Kaiser. He was exceptionally reticent in speaking about his war experiences. The only information I ever got from him was so interlaced with new and strange execrations that it was of no use to me.

I remember that Harold stated one time, "a bayonet was hard to pull out, even when you put your foot on his face," but otherwise, he contributed little of value in my views on the war. I judged that Harold had spent an exciting period at the front until he connected with a German "minnewerfer"* which caved in the dug-out and his chest. He recuperated in the hospital until discharged to Canada. He retained, as a souvenir, a bad case of insomnia, a pulse of 112, a tendency to exhaustion, and what he colloquially termed as "a pain in my gut." *Editor's Note: "Minnewerfer" is the name for a short range* *mortar shell used during the First World War by the German Army.*

George, Harold and I rode a narrow valley for ten or twelve miles. The valley had been burned over and was full of dead and fallen timber. It was extremely tough going. The sides and bottom were filled with fallen logs, and in the center was a roaring torrent of water, swollen by the melting snow. We proceeded about ten to twelve miles and set up our tent on a little flat area which afforded some feed for our horses. The stream ran near our tent. I was able to fly fish wherever a log gave protection from the faster current and had no difficulty in catching several trout to add to our food.

The mountains rose steeply on each side of the valley and were covered with burnt and green timber topped by granite cliffs and peaks covered with snow. It was evidently an ideal country for mountain goats. We could see them wandering up and down the higher slopes of the mountains at almost any time.

## Rockslides

Higher up the same valley, at various points on the mountainside, the timber had been swept away by avalanches of past years, leaving the earth bare. There were patches of grass and willows, and whenever they were exposed to the sun, they appeared green and dotted with yellow lilies. At this time in the spring, there was little or nothing growing in the timber.

A grizzly bear could come out upon these slides to feed on the green growth. The only method of hunting a grizzly was to search various rockslides with my glasses to see whether any bear appeared.

## The Gale

For three days, George and I worked up and down the valley, climbing over dead timber and pushing through muskeg swamps without seeing any signs of a grizzly. The third night when we returned to camp, the wind began to rise. By the time darkness arrived, it was blowing like a hurricane. The noise of the gale almost drowned the steady roar of the creek on which we were camped.

Every few moments, the crashing of falling timber sounded like the thunder of artillery. At times, one tree would fall with a crash, and then there would be a loud volley as if the whole forest had fallen together.

We were camped in the open under one big dead tree. I awoke in the night and wondered whether the tree would fall on me. The high wind would last until morning, and the horses had sense enough to get out of the timber. In the morning when we awakened, the horses were gone. It was evident that they did not like the gale and had decided to clear out. George felt that he was the only one who could find the horses and started walking back toward his ranch.

## Bears

In the meantime, Harold and I thought we would go up the valley to watch the slides for bears at the upper end and have lunch. I took my rifle, and Harold put a teapot, two cups, our sweaters, and my camera in a small pack sack, and we started walking.

The storm had made the valley even harder going than before. Climbing over downed timber is hard work, and we could not go faster than two miles an hour. After we had gone about three miles, we found an open place where we could see both sides of the valley. We sat down and watched the various slides.

Noon came, and we made tea and were drinking it when Harold put down his cup and took up the field glasses focusing on a slide on the other side of the valley. He announced that he could see a bear and thought it was a grizzly. I took the glasses and had no difficulty in seeing this bear which was feeding on a small patch of lilies in an opening in the willows. After careful inspection, we were convinced that this bear was a full-grown grizzly.

Harold and I were on one side of the valley while the bear was on the other, and the creek was running high and fast between us. We went up and down the creek looking for a place to cross, but it seemed impossible. The stream was one solid roaring mass of white water. It was evident that no one could swim in it nor keep his on his feet trying to ford it.

The only place where it could possibly be crossed was just above our camp. At that location, there was an enormous log jam which had fallen over the stream. It seemed like it might be a simple matter to cross over it while stepping carefully on the logs. This would mean a long detour and the possibility that the grizzly might disappear. There was no other way to cross the water. We reluctantly packed up the tea pot, cups, our sweaters and my camera.

### Danger!

Harold and I started walking toward the log jam in the stream  We had gone about a half mile from the camp when we came to an island in the middle of the stream with a big log jam spanning the further branch. Two small logs reached from our side to the island. Harold said he thought we should cross here and save a lot of time. He started out by walking with one foot on each log. When he got about ten feet from the shore, one of the logs bent until it touched the water. Instantly the water swept over it. I saw Harold's foot slip, and he fell backward into the water toward me. When he struck the water, he caught a log with one hand and got a leg over the second log to keep from being swept under the fast-moving current. The water rose in a wave over Harold's body, submerging everything but his face. He was nearly swept under the logs.

I laid my rifle down on the bank and crawled out a little way on the logs to where Harold was trapped. Fortunately, he had fallen close to shore, so I had no trouble getting to him. First, I took hold of his shoulders with both my hands and tried to lift him, but he was pinned solidly as if he was caught in a vice. I could not move Harold at all. I worked feverishly and desperately for several minutes trying to help him but could not give him the slightest relief from his terrible predicament. In fact, the only thing I seemed able to do was to support his head so that the water would not break over his face and strangle him.

I do not know how long I worked to help him. I began to feel that if I did not do something quickly, the continual current of icy water pouring over Harold would exhaust him. The painful expression on his face showed that he was nearing the end of his strength. I knew that if he let go of the log, I could not hold him. Harold would be swept downstream and drowned beyond a doubt. I remember thinking that it seemed such a pity that a man who could survive the War in

France would drown in a fourth-class creek in Canada.

Harold kept trying to say something to me, but I could not hear his words above the roaring of the water. Twice I asked him if he could possibly duck under the logs and come up on the other side. Harold shook his head, but I am not sure he understood me. Finally, he called out so loudly that I heard him say, "For God's sake, get the pack off my back!" I had to decide quickly what I was going to do next to help Harold.

## My Knife

I reached in my pocket for my knife only to find that I did not have it with me. I believe in twenty years of hunting I have lugged around more useless hardware than any man in America without ever wanting a knife as badly as I did at that moment. For the only time in my history, I could not believe it as I didn't have my knife. Harold started to let go with one hand to reach for his own knife and in doing so, was almost swept away.

Something had to be done immediately. I reached down and got hold of Harold's pack straps and pulled with all my strength. During my first attempt, I ripped Harold's suspenders from him, buttons and all. Fortunately, on my second attempt, I burst the sewing of his pack straps away from the pack and tore it all loose. I lifted the crossed straps over his head and let go of the pack sack. I never thought that I was separating myself from the teapot, cups, our sweaters, and my camera. Nothing was ever seen of that pack sack again.

This explains why this story was not profusely illustrated with photographs taken on the spot. Even if we still had the camera,

I doubt whether Harold or I would have had any time for taking pictures.

Relieved from the weight of Harold's pack sack, I was finally able to move and pull him gradually up on top of the water and logs and back on to shore. Harold's face and hands were blue with cold and exhaustion. He complained of feeling sick and lightheaded.

Nevertheless, after a few minutes, Harold was able to walk back to camp by his own strength and legs. Once there, he took off his wet clothes and crawled into his bed covered with blankets. I made a fire, heated a pot of tea and filled him up with it. As soon as he began to warm up from the hot tea and the blankets, I turned my attention once more to hunting the grizzly bear.

## Bear Hunting

Harold was exhausted but anxious to have me go bear hunting. Even with his narrow escape, Harold felt there was no reason why I should stay in camp with him. I grabbed my rifle and glasses and set off. I carefully crossed over the log jam (the reader can feel certain that I took no chances of falling into the water) and started walking up the other side of the valley. For three miles I climbed up and down over fallen logs and pushed through thick willow brush until I came to the spot where I thought I had first seen the grizzly.

Two narrow slides came down the mountain at this point  Each was a mixture of willow brush and open spaces with a little ridge between them. The grizzly bear was not in sight. I thought, of course, that he had probably disappeared for the day. However,

I intended to spend until dark waiting for him. I would go to one of the slides, sit down and watch for fifteen minutes and then walk over to the next slide and do the same thing.

After about an hour and a half, I suddenly spotted a bear walking out on one of the slides about a half mile above me and begin to feed. I looked him over with the glasses, and he seemed to be a full-grown grizzly bear. While he was the first grizzly I had ever seen in natural surroundings, he appeared to me exactly as I had expected a grizzly bear would look. I threw a cartridge into the barrel of my Springfield rifle, examined the sights to see if they were in proper shape, and started walking up toward him.

When I got within two hundred yards of the bear, he was feeding right at the edge of some willows. I was afraid he would walk away and disappear into the willows. I didn't want to wait any longer, so I laid down, took careful aim, held my breath, and fired at him. The grizzly was on a steep hillside. At the crack of my rifle, he went struggling and kicking down the slope. I threw another cartridge into the barrel, but before I could shoot, the bear got to his feet and made one quick jump disappearing into the brush. I climbed up as rapidly as possible to the spot where I thought he might be.

However, I was reluctant to rush into the brush and try to drag him out by the tail as a wounded bear could be dangerous. I carefully worked around the ridge where I could see into the willows and make sure that he had not laid down immediately. Afterwards, I followed the grizzly up over a ridge but could find no traces of him.

The country, at that point, was a perfect tangle of downed timber and willow brush extending for miles. There were no tracks or blood to show whether this bear had gone up or down the ridge. I was unable to follow him. As the grizzly was showing his side to me when I pulled the trigger, there is no doubt in my mind that my shot went far back through the bear's guts. The only reason the grizzly got knocked down was the fact that he was standing on a steep hillside.

Any wounded animal can go for miles before he finally dies. The saddest part of it is that after being hit with the umbrella pointed Springfield bullet, there is not the slightest chance of this bear ever recovering from the wound. I had to acknowledge that I had done a poor job shooting him.

I returned to camp to find Harold feeling much better and not much worse for his harrowing experience. The next day, George arrived back in camp with the horses. Then George, Harold and I searched the slide area again for the wounded grizzly bear without success. I had no doubt that the bear's body was lying somewhere in the downed timber of the valley.

As a consolation, I could look at Harold's weather-beaten and good-natured countenance and feel as if the good Lord had made me make my choice between Harold and the grizzly. I was so lucky to have him alive. Hip, Hip Hooray for Harold!

*The Call of Lonely Places*
By Phillip Arnold La Vie

*Billow on rolling billow*
*Each with its foaming crest,*
*Seeming to ceaselessly beckon,*
*Calling in vague unrest.*

*Ever its restless bosom,*
*Rolling in long dark swells,*
*Rises in emerald mountains,*

*Sinks into sea green dells.*
*Ever its misty headlands*
*Fade into filmy grey,*
*Ever the sound of its breakers,*
*Thunders and dies away.*

\* \* \* \*

*Land of the sportsman's fancy,*
*Waters untried by rod,*
*Distance that knows no trespass*
*Saving the hand of God;*
*Barren and bleak and lonely,*
*Waiting the Pioneer,*
*Ruled by the power of the Red Gods,*
*Silent and deep and austere.*
*Land of the open spaces,*
*Far from the cold world's hum,*
*Land of the Lone, you call me,*
*Land of the Free, I come!*

**The End**

Big Game Hunting Tales        Russell Mott

Big Game Hunting Tales  Russell Mott

# **A Healthy Appetite**

### **By Double Barrel**

There is nothing more important in the world than the contents of one's stomach, and arguing from that premise, the contents of other stomachs should also be of interest. Hence, here is the following account:

Last spring, we were anchored in a gasoline cruiser in the Bay of Honda off the Florida Keys waiting for the weather to turn warm enough for the tarpon to bite. Meanwhile, we amused ourselves by fishing for other fish and catching lobsters and stone crabs for the dinner table.

Shark Lines

Captain Jim had set out a couple of shark lines which he attached to some old pilings which had been laid by the Florida East Coast Railroad at the time of its construction. These wood pilings floated above the water in certain parts of the Bay. These lines were about one hundred feet of five-eighths inch manila rope at the end of which was three or four feet of chain with hooks baited with three or four pounds of. any uneatable fish we happened to have on hand.

From the deck of the boat, we could see up the shark lines through my glasses and could see whether they were entirely free or not. The first day we had the lines out, we caught a small shark weighing perhaps one hundred pounds.

The next day, we were fortunate to catch a saw fish, fourteen feet with a forty-four-inch saw.

## Leopard Shark

On the third day, about three o'clock in the afternoon, we saw that the shark line which was in the middle of the channel of the Bay, was taut. Four of us got into one of the small motorboats to go over to it. I carried my thirty-forty rifle. When we arrived at the line, the boat captain and a crew member gradually hauled it in until they pulled the head of a large shark out of the water. As soon as the head was above the surface, I shot the shark twice through the head which finished his career. We hauled him into the boat, and the next question was what to do with such a big shark.

Inspection showed that he was a very large leopard shark which the natives insisted was a man-eater. His jaws were armed with an interesting set of teeth consisting of six rows, one inside the other. I suggested that I would like to cut out the jaws and keep them as souvenir. Eventually, we pulled this leopard shark up onto the beach and measured him at a little over nine feet long. We tried to weigh him on the davits before landing him, but our scales would not accommodate more than six hundred pounds. He was much heavier than that, and we were unable to get his actual weight.

## Shark's Stomach

We cut him open as I was anxious to see what was inside of him. His internal apparatus was surprisingly simple. Apparently, he had little to boast of in the way of organs except his stomach and liver. This shark's stomach was like an enormous flour sack. On each side, there were two enormous layers of liver extending the whole length of his body and about one and half feet across.

When the shark's stomach was cut open, we found the most extraordinary collection of objects imaginable. To begin with, there were the remains of a dozen lobsters, at least what is known as lobsters along the Florida Keys. These lobsters were much larger than the ones caught in the North and had two long feelers and no pinchers. There were nine of these lobsters. Some of these were entirely undigested with the remains of four or five in different stages of degeneration. In many cases, the lobsters' shells were almost totally digested.

Besides the lobsters, there was a ten-pound horse-shoe crab and a moray eel which is a saltwater snake about five feet long. There were also several pelican feathers with the heavy wing feathers being entirely intact although the rest of the bird had been totally digested. As the pelican slowly rises from the water, I have no doubt that the shark had succeeded in seizing it a similar manner to a trout grabbing a fly on the surface of the water.

In addition to these items, we also found about 100 pieces of tortoise shell, evidently the remains of a large Hawksbill Turtle. Of this collection of tortoise shell, some of the flakes were six inches long by four inches wide and digested so that they had become about as thin as cardboard. Several flakes I picked out of the miscellaneous debris of the shark's stomach and brought home with me to vouch for the truth of this story. I provided one piece of them to *Forest and Stream Magazine*.

There was no meat or anything of that kind in the stomach of this shark. I do not believe that a fish could be swallowed without being digested, bones and all. After thoroughly examining the shark's stomach, we cut out the jaws and discovered a peculiarity of construction. This shark could swallow almost anything. The jaws were not only joined at the side but also in the center with heavy cartilages so they could be spread open wide to any position or shape to accommodate any sized object. The jaws were equipped with six rows of teeth. The inner five were flat while the upper row was upright and were adapted for cutting. I have no doubt that the other rows of teeth could be raised on necessity or perhaps were intended to take the place of any of the forward ones which became broken.

The contents of our friend's stomach would certainly seem natural when one considers that a shark's jaws are set not under his nose but under his chin. To take an object on the surface, the shark must turn almost completely over to grab it. It would, therefore, be much simpler and easier for him to take most of his food under the water or from the bottom.

It would be interesting to know whether the contents of this shark's stomach is a fair sample, or whether this would be an unusual one. It would seem, however, that the turtle the shark devoured must have been eighteen inches to two feet across its back. Such a big morsel would not come to a shark every day.

The next day, our longest shark line attached to a piling was broken off by something extremely large, probably another big shark. On the following day, we left for other fishing grounds where sharks might be more plentiful but never caught another as large as that leopard shark.

## The End

## Afterword: My Ancestors

My grandfather, Russell Mott, attended Harvard and became an attorney in Chicago. He hunted big game in Canada, lower California, and Africa. I knew him slightly, when at five years old, I visited his farm near Charlottesville, VA where he and my grandmother, Helen Cutler, retired.

The farm was an idyllic place as the countryside was so beautiful. There was a large expansive home with two servants, a cook and a farm hand who lived on the property. The property included a barn, a separate building for my grandfather's hunting rifles, antique pistols, and mounted game heads, and a kennel with many fox hounds.

I remember him riding his horse nattily attired in a long red coat blowing a horn to start a fox hunt as the dogs barked excitedly. My grandfather was an individualist and would not join the local fox hunting club. He purchased young fox pups that were let go at specific locations until they could mature and be available to hunt. His domestic dog choice was an English bulldog named Mick. Russell wrote several hunting articles using both his own name and the pseudonym "Double Barrel" for *Forest and Stream* Magazine which I have included in this book.

Russell and his wife, Helen Cutler, had four children, John Grenville (my father), Evelyn, Cutler, and Joseph. Tragically, almost the whole family was wiped out by alcohol addiction. First, my grandfather died from the disease. My father, his sister, Evelyn, and his brother, Cutler, all died from alcohol abuse. Their younger brother, Joe, graduated from Yale with a law degree, married and had a child, and then committed suicide due to mental illness. I am proud to say that both my sister, Sheridan, and I broke the cycle and do not drink alcohol.

My grandfather, Russell aka "Double Barrel," and his father and my great grandfather, John G. Mott, who wrote *Monarch of the Glen*, were both exceptional writers. I am so pleased that I could transcribe, edit and publish these 100+ year-old big hunting adventures for you. What treasures I found!

Warmest regards,

**Graham M. Mott,** grandson of Russell Mott, transcriber, editor, publisher, and author.

## More books from Golden Shadows Press:

**Hooked by Fly Fishing**

Feel-Good Stories of Family and Friends, Life Lessons, Mishaps, and Mayhem

**Graham M. Mott**

**Monarch of the Glen**

A True Adventure Story of a Big Game Hunt in Wyoming - 1900

John G. Mott
transcribed and edited by his great grandson, Graham M. Mott, author of "Hooked by Fly Fishing"

**More Big Game Hunting Tales**

from the early 1900s

by Russell Mott
aka "Double Barrel"
Transcribed & edited by his grandson,
Graham M. Mott, author of "Hooked by Fly Fishing."

**Available as paperbacks or eBooks at Amazon.com**

www.ingramcontent.com/pod-product-compliance
Ingram Content Group UK Ltd.
Pitfield, Milton Keynes, MK11 3LW, UK
UKHW040857240225
455493UK00001B/33